Lot American el.

CP 15^u

Dearest Andrew

Dearest Andrew

LETTERS FROM
 V. SACKVILLE-WEST
TO
ANDREW REIBER, 1951–1962

EDITED BY NANCY MacKNIGHT

CHARLES SCRIBNER'S SONS / NEW YORK

Copyright © 1979 Andrew Reiber and Nancy MacKnight

Library of Congress Cataloging in Publication Data

Sackville-West, Victoria Mary, Hon., 1892–1962.
  Dearest Andrew.

  Letters of Victoria Mary Sackville-West to Andrew
Reiber.
  Bibliography: p. 127.
    1. Sackville-West, Victoria Mary, Hon., 1892–1962—
Correspondence.   2. Authors, English—20th century—
Correspondence.   3. Reiber, Andrew.   I. Reiber,
Andrew.   II. MacKnight, Nancy.   III. Title.
PR6037.A35Z495   823'.9'12   79-9244
ISBN 0-684-16275-X

Extracts from *Diaries and Letters* by Harold Nicolson reprinted by permission of Collins
Publishers, London; the broadcast *This I Believe* by V. Sackville-West by permission of
Curtis Brown Ltd., London; *Britain's Rose Queen* by Gordon Langley Hall, reprinted
courtesy of the *Boston Globe*; material from *Journey to Java* by Harold Nicolson by
permission of Constable Publishers, London; letters and poems by V. Sackville-West by
permission of Nigel Nicolson.

BY ANDREW'S WISH,

THIS BOOK IS DEDICATED TO

THE MEMORY OF

ACKNOWLEDGMENTS

I am indebted to Mr. Nigel Nicolson, not only for his permission to publish these letters, poems, and pictures, but also for his cooperation and support throughout the writing of the book.

I would also like to thank Michel and Ingrid Chalufour of Addison, Maine, who introduced me to Andrew Reiber.

N. M.

CONTENTS

Dearest Andrew

Foreword

WELL-WRITTEN LETTERS, no matter how ordinary the day-to-day activities they chronicle, are fascinating to read. The correspondence between Vita Sackville-West and Andrew Reiber did not generally deal with matters of moment. It recorded the weather, always a topic of great concern to gardeners, the welfare of flowers or of dogs, and a multitude of human kindnesses generously offered and graciously received.

V. Sackville-West was an unusual combination of a public and a private person. She guarded her privacy at Sissinghurst fiercely and resented the intrusion even of close friends. Yet in her books, her novels, and her poems, she candidly presented herself for the world to read. Also paradoxically, she welcomed people to come and enjoy the exquisite garden she had created at Sissinghurst. In 1945 she wrote to her husband, the diplomat and writer Harold Nicolson: "Quite a lot of people have been to see the garden, which always pleases me. How much I prefer strangers to my friends."[1] This is not the place nor is there time to delve into the reasons for such a statement. Suffice it to say that her friendship in letters with Andrew Reiber, a congenial personality but still a stranger, who lived halfway around the world in a land of fabled natural beauty, appealed to her romantic nature. The bond may have been strengthened by the fact that it was unlikely ever to be tried by a personal encounter.

During Vita's lifetime, her name was well known to a wide reading audience, particularly for her novels of the 1930s, *The Edwardians* and *All Passion Spent*. After her death in 1962, her works rapidly went out of print. Although not a writer of genius, she was beyond doubt a professional, turning out a substantial number of books, as well as journalistic assignments, pamphlets, introductions, and a host of horticultural articles. With the publication, in 1973, of her son's edition of the autobiographical fragment that she had written many years before her death, the spotlight of the literary world was suddenly thrown upon her once again. The title *Portrait of a Marriage* is somewhat misleading, as the main episode spans the years 1918 to 1921, when the young Vita's lesbian passion for Violet Trefusis, her friend from childhood, was at its height. The book does discuss the solid and particularly loving marriage that Vita and Harold Nicolson achieved, but it dismisses her later years in a somewhat perfunctory fashion. True, her activity as a writer had decreased considerably by the time she was sixty, but her life continued to be many faceted and productive.

The letters in the present volume provide a glimpse of an aspect of Vita seldom seen in public—the thoughtful, affectionate friend. On occasion she wrote to her unknown "dearest Andrew" of surprisingly intimate things, for his was a sympathetic ear that heard her always in the most favorable way. Their friendship demanded little materially of her, beyond the time it took to scribble friendly little letters seven or eight times a year. To read these letters is to understand Vita's day-to-day existence, and to see her for the patient, loving person she was. The stormy, arrogant side of her character is not denied, but these letters give us more evidence with which to interpret her complex personality.

The photograph of Vita that stands on Andrew's table. *Courtesy of* The Observer.

My aim in presenting this correspondence is to let Vita's words stand on their own. I have tried to prevent my comments from intruding on her own expression. Therefore I have limited my remarks to necessary narrative or explanation and have avoided interpretation. From these pages I hope the reader will receive an undiluted and unbiased picture of Vita, in all her generosity, idiosyncrasy, snobbishness, and joie de vivre. Andrew remains a somewhat shadowy figure, more so to the reader than he was for Vita, who could know him through his lovingly composed letters. This is as Andrew wishes, since he sees this book of their correspondence as primarily Vita's. It is his tribute to a heart that had room for simple friendship as well as passionate love. At the time of this writing Andrew lives happily at Windslip, among his memories of the past and his many devoted friends. Vita's photograph stands on the table of his sitting room. Her memory is cherished at Windslip to this day.

Acquaintanceship

1951–1954

VITA SACKVILLE-WEST received dozens of letters each week. She answered every one, but even with the help of a secretary, it was a formidable task. She often sighed, when she sat down to the pile of letters, to think that her gardening articles, published weekly in the *Observer*, were bringing her the popular recognition never accorded to her poetry, the writing that meant most to her. Nonetheless, it was impossible not to be touched by the warm reception that her readers were giving her casual, sometimes humorous, sometimes stern, advice on gardening.

On March 31, 1951, Vita was just getting over a case of flu, a malady that people who live in drafty castles such as Sissinghurst may contract more readily than others. The worst of the attack had passed, and she could once more climb the steep steps of her Elizabethan tower to her study to continue her various writing chores, among them the inevitable letters from her gardening admirers. On this particular day there was a fat en-

velope postmarked in the United States, with a return address
that must have appealed to her romantic imagination—
"Windslip, Cape Split, Maine." The writer, Andrew Reiber,
knew her works well. Her interest in his letter may have been
piqued by the fact that he had been reading her poetry, her
novels, and her essays for years before the *Observer* articles
thrust her into new prominence. Then, too, he was not writing
a mere fan letter, solely to express his admiration for her gardening lore or to ask her the solution to a thorny gardening problem. Instead, he explained about a young American, Thomas
Merriam, the son of his dear friend Ann Merriam. Tom was
attending Tonbridge School, not far from the village of Cran-
brook where Sissinghurst is situated. He was engaged on a special study of the architecture of Tudor Kent. Might he then visit
Sissinghurst Castle and see the remains of the sixteenth-century
buildings that Vita and her husband Harold Nicolson had saved
from ruin and transformed into one of the most beautiful,
though unusual, dwellings in England? Such a civil request
made it easy for Vita to frame her reply. In her meticulous
hand, she wrote:

Dear Mr. Reiber

Many thanks for your letter—it is funny to think of my
Observer articles finding their way out to Maine! I have
always heard that Maine was very beautiful, especially in
the autumn.

I should be very pleased to see your friend's son here; it
is not much good my writing to him at Tonbridge School
now as they will be having their Easter holidays—so
perhaps your friend would tell him to come when it suits
him. The garden is open daily, and I am usually here—so
he can ask for me. If, as you say, he is writing about

Vita at Sissinghurst with Rollo in the early 1950s. The window of her tower study shows clearly. *Courtesy of Nigel Nicolson.*

Tudor Kent, he should certainly come to Sissinghurst, as this house dates from 1540.

You will understand, I am sure, that I am a busy person and that it is difficult for me to make engagements, but if he will just turn up I will be very glad to see him.

Yours sincerely,
V. Sackville-West

There was something distinctly attractive to Vita in the thought of an unknown man, far away on the coast of Maine, reading and responding intelligently to her work. She found it difficult to put the letter down, and some impulse made her add a helpful postscript: "By the way, there was an illustrated article in the American edition of *House and Garden* last autumn, on Sissinghurst. Perhaps you could get hold of a copy?"

Her attention must have been distracted for a moment from her writing; perhaps she was called away from her desk. Something prevented her from slipping the sheet of writing paper into its envelope and sealing it. Before she did so, she took another sheet and scrawled on it: "I continue this letter, just to say that I nearly called my eldest son Andrew—born in August 1914—two days after the war broke out. I thought it such a nice name—and it was a family name in my family, right back into 1200 A.D. Look, I must stop writing—I have things to see to —household things—so goodbye."

When this letter made its way across the Atlantic to the picturesque seaside village of Addison where Windslip is located, Andrew Reiber read it with delight. For years, in reading Vita's published work, he had sensed a bond, a common interest. Andrew is something of a mystic and believes in links between people, sometimes people from totally different backgrounds. This letter, which she was loath to close, certainly seemed to indicate her own sense of such an affinity.

Andrew's home, Windslip, was, for its own time and coun-

Andrew at Windslip in 1952. *Courtesy of Mrs. Wallace Dickson.*

try, as elegant and distinctive as Sissinghurst. Addison had been a working fishing village since the time it was first settled early in the seventeenth century. In the 1930s, it enjoyed something of a vogue among the inhabitants of the artistic world. The painter John Marin made his home there. Writers, musicians, and theatre people found their way to Cape Split, just outside the town. Among them were Walter Sinclair, a producer and director, and his companion Andrew Reiber, an actor. For sev-

Views of the garden at Windslip. *Courtesy of Alicia Rogan Heard.*

eral seasons they took houses in Addison or one of the surrounding villages. Then, in 1939, they discovered Windslip, a cottage
dating back to Revolutionary times. It was nearly past repair,
but with careful planning and attention to historical accuracy,
the two men had it restored to its original beauty. Overlooking
the sea, the cottage stands on a rise, amid ancient apple trees. A
long meadow stretches down to the curve of a sandy beach on
one side. Behind the house, formal gardens give way to pine
woods through which one reaches another strand set off by mas-
sive rocks on either side. When Walter Sinclair retired from the
theatre, the two friends took up permanent residence in this
beautiful spot. There they could read and write, surrounded by
nourishing natural beauty and attended by their aristocratic

standard poodles. They were almost undisturbed during the winter, but in the summer innumerable friends, no matter where they lived and worked, found their way to this idyllic spot for at least a few days each year.

Andrew had no doubt that Vita's letter required a reply. He sensed in it the same sympathy that had come to him whenever he read her work. In his next letter he put news of the quaint life around him on the Maine coast, as well as his appreciation for Vita's willingness to receive young Tom. There was no need for her to answer Andrew. A letter now would, after all, be a reply to a reply. Andrew waited in eager anticipation throughout 1951 to discover whether or not his sense of a bond was valid. It was not until November 5 that Vita wrote again.

The St. Francis shrine.
Courtesy of Alicia Rogan Heard.

Rear view of Windslip.
Courtesy of Mrs. Wallace Dickson.

The side beach at Windslip. *Courtesy of Michel Chalufour.*

The view from Windslip's side windows. *Courtesy of Michel Chalufour.*

Dear Mr. Reiber,

I have been a dreadfully long time answering your letter, but it was only this morning that I discovered an old copy of the American edition of House and Garden and found that it was November 1950 with the article on Sissinghurst.

I am sure that the autumn colouring in Maine must be wonderful just now: I have always heard about it and hope some day to see it.

I never heard any more from your young friend at Tonbridge School or I would of course have asked him to come over.

I loved your story about the wife of the lobster fisherman and the Vita seat, but I was puzzled by the word 'jog-tow' and do hope that you will tell me some day what it means.

Meanwhile may I send you both my good wishes for Christmas although that seems rather far ahead.

Yours sincerely,
V. Sackville-West

This businesslike letter was one of the few typewritten ones that Andrew ever received during the eleven years of their correspondence. Had he been a man of slightly less faith and enthusiasm, he no doubt would never have answered this formal, somewhat chilly letter. But he did, and in so doing made his best effort, what he terms his "creative writing." The magic was restored. Surely his letter conjured up his own particular world for Vita's benefit and strengthened the bond that was evident to them both in Andrew's first letter. This time Vita's reply was immediate. It came on a Christmas card of Sissinghurst and opened with:

Dear friend Andrew   Dec. 27, 1951

Your letter has just come—I wish I could send you a bottle of that sovereign remedy Sloan's liniment to cure your stiff neck. Do they sell it in U.S.A.? If so, I recommend it for all aches of that sort.

As I can't send you a bottle, I've asked my publishers to send you a little book of mine instead, just as a Christmas card.

Oh yes, I would like to see your farm and the lovely Maine country—Harold knows it, but I don't.

Fog-bow . . . I must apologise for having misread you. How beautiful it must have been. I think that MIST-Bow would be a prettier name. Fog is such an ugly word and can be such an ugly thing. The white mist of the country places is a lovely, imaginative thing (so long as you don't have to drive a motor car in it) but fog to us so often means the murky dark of London, which is anything but beautiful.

I am going to ask a favour of you. I hope you won't mind: I feel pretty sure you won't. It is something I covet passionately for my garden. It is a packet of seeds —Bodgers' Zinnias—the stripy ones. The seed is unobtainable here, and is the envy of every gardener. The American firm called Bodgers sell them—so I imagine that you could easily buy a packet of seed and post them to me. I can't send you any money to pay for them, because we

are not allowed to send money out of this country, but I can get some American stamps, and I will send you those—and if you would really get me a packet of seed I would grow them in your honour.

It is interesting to speculate on the reasons that Vita, a woman of infinite resources, with multitudes of connections all over the world, should ask a stranger, a man with whom she had exchanged three letters, to send her seed of a coveted plant. Certainly, the situation appealed to her romantic temperament —the unknown friend, someone she would never meet, about whom all sorts of fantasies might be erected. Andrew gave ample opportunity for the building of such fantasies. He lived in an exotic spot; he knew flowers and books; he loved words and expressed himself easily and well. Above all, he admired Vita with a genuine admiration that did not depend on critics' notices or the ratings of the best sellers. There is no question that such a mysterious romantic relationship intrigued Vita, as she was to mention many times in years to come.

Andrew responded to Vita's request as would a knight to a sacred trust. He dispatched letters to major seed dealers all over the country. He even wrote to the illustrious Dr. L. H. Bailey at the Bailey Hortorium of Cornell University in an attempt to trace the exact seed for which Vita asked. He almost immediately bought some seed from Burnett Brothers in New York and mailed them to Vita.

Within ten days of her original request's reaching Andrew, Vita had possession of a quarter-ounce of Bodgers Peppermint Stick Zinnias. Her thank-you letter to Andrew was swift and graceful.

My dear friend Andrew   January 26, 1952

Imagine my excitement when on a snowy morning your letter arrived with the precious seeds inside. How can I thank you? Only by telling you that they will be cherished and cossetted, and each one grown separately in its own small pot until the moment comes for planting them out. Then a necklace of slugbait will be put round each.

I am sending you, as a very inadequate return, a little book in which you will find something about zinnias, p. 207.[2] I do not think I have sent you this little book before, but if so please forgive me. The photographs in the book, by the way, are of my own garden (except, of course, the ones of Hidcote Manor.) Look at the frontispiece: The first floor window in the tower is my sitting room where I am writing this.

How I wish you could come here! Not at the moment, though, for it is very cold and snowy, and we have only wood fires, no central heating, which I am sure must sound most barbarous to American ears. I expect it is

(29)

pretty cold in Maine too, but at least you keep warm indoors. Now I must thank you again, but more than I can
say, and take my leave of you with boundless gratitude.

Vita

Andrew's several requests to seed companies resulted in the
arrival of another package on Vita's doorstep on February 14.
The happy coincidence of the date was to make the observation
of Valentine's Day a special holiday for Andrew and Vita. That
particular February was specially fraught for Vita and Harold
and the entire British people. King George VI had died unexpectedly at Sandringham on the morning of February 6. On
that same day, the citizens of Bournemouth were to vote for
their new Member of Parliament. Nigel Nicolson, Vita's
younger son, was standing as candidate for the Conservative
Party. Amidst the confusion caused by the death of the king,
Nigel was elected to office.

February 14, 1952

My dear Andrew

Another great huge packet of seed! How marvellous
—and how kind of you. I am now planning to have a
whole border (narrow, but very long) entirely filled with
your zinnias. And look at the date on which they arrived:
St. Valentine's day, which the birds at any rate think is the
first day of spring. (Do you in America also observe St.
Valentine's day?) I can't say it is much like spring here,
because it is snowing, but neither that nor anything else
can diminish my delight in the seeds.

We are sad about our King, but nobody has anything
but praise for our young Queen.

(30)

My son has just become a member of Parliament, which is fun for him.

Well, I must thank you again—and oh by the way, the day after I had posted my letter to you I got one from you saying that I *had* already sent you my little garden book —so I won't burden you with another copy.

> Yours very very gratefully
> Vita

The long-distance friendship was cemented by this time. The "Andrew zinnias" were germinating; Andrew was storing up tales of the Maine countryside and its inhabitants with which to entertain Vita.

Some months passed before her next letter came.

July 20, 1952

Oh, dear Andrew, I have been a terribly long time in answering your last letter. Every day I have meant to sit down and answer it, and always somebody or something came to interrupt. Still, there is some compensation in this delay, because I can now tell you that the Andrew zinnias (as I call them) are beginning to flower—and very lovely they are—so varied in their stripings and flakings and colourings—and very exciting to us who have never grown them before. I promise you that all the trouble you went to in getting the seed is being richly rewarded at this end. Every day I see a new one come out, and it is always different, and I can't thank you enough: they are a real pride to my garden. No one else has them!

I am sending you, in a separate packet, some new

photograph-postcards of the garden here. I am sorry that
the Andrew zinnias are not shown on them, but of course
the photographs were taken long before the seeds came up.
There is not even a photograph of the place where they are
growing, which is along the foot of a very long wall of pink
Tudor brick, broken at intervals by stone piers. It is the
ideal place for them, I think: the rosy background of the
old brick suits them to perfection.

We get a lot of visitors to the garden, and many Americans amongst them,—more this year than ever before. I
am always so glad to see them, remembering the kindness
and hospitality I met with on my visit to the States in
1933. I never got to Maine! though, as I think I told you,
Harold has been there, to stay with Mrs. Dwight Morrow
when he was writing the life of her husband.

We follow your Presidential elections with the deepest
interest, and watch the films of conferences on the television. Did I tell you that my youngest son is now a
Member of Parliament? It does seem so odd, when I still
think of him as a little boy—and a very untidy little boy at
that, with his shirt always hanging out of his trousers.

Well, dear Andrew, I must say goodbye but please write
to me again.

> Your distant but affectionate friend
> Vita

This letter is typical of the correspondence of the next ten
years. Vita, with so many daily duties and activities, was almost
always behind in her letter writing. She would usually open
with regrets for taking so long to reply to Andrew. She would
then give him some news of the garden and of her private life.

Vita's 1952 Christmas card, the Vestal Virgin statue in the garden at Sissinghurst. *Courtesy of E. A. Sweetman and Son, Ltd.*

(33)

She hardly ever mentioned the books on which she was at work or the politics that concerned her husband and her son Nigel. She might sometimes remark on her life with Harold or interject his point of view, particularly when it was at odds with her own. There might be a reference to some small gift for Andrew or to her appreciation of one from him. Often she would refer to the strangeness of their friendship—stressing the fact that although they had never met, nor were likely to, they had so many interests in common. Her Christmas card to Andrew that year suggests this aspect of their unusual relationship. On the front is a photograph of a statue. Inside, under the traditional greeting, Vita wrote: "This is a photograph of a statue in my garden. The sculptor called her 'The Vestal Virgin.' She stands under a grey-leaved tree in a grey-and-white garden and she comes to wish you a very happy Christmas although she has never met you."

The following year, 1953, was a rewarding and satisfying one for the Nicolsons, both professionally and personally. Vita had finished her novel *The Easter Party* the previous year and it was published in January. Its appearance was a significant event for her, because for the previous few years her writing had been blocked. She had confided in Harold her agony at being unable to write. When her novel began to unfurl under her pen, she experienced immense relief and satisfaction. In December 1950, she wrote to her husband:

Darling, I must write you another little note just to say how happy I am writing. It does make the whole difference in life. I just tell you this, because I like sharing things with you. I have been so miserable in the last two or three years, not being able to write; really worried I have been, thinking it was gone from me forever. I don't mean by this that I think my novel [*The Easter Party*] will be any good—you know that I am not a good novelist—but at any rate it is exciting just doing it. It keeps me alive, living in an imaginary world which seems more real than the ordinary world. Of course I would rather write poetry. Perhaps that will also return to me one day.[3]

This book represented a victory of Vita's spirit. Such ups and downs in writing were not so familiar to Harold as they were to Vita. His monumental biography of King George V had appeared in 1952, and his name was included on the list for New Year's Day honors the following year. The queen rewarded his labors with a K. C. V. O.[4] Previously, Harold Nicolson had been against accepting such honors, but to refuse the K. C. V. O. would have been churlish, he thought, so he became a knight.

Uncharacteristically, Andrew did not answer Vita's Christmas card until February of 1953. However, the envelope, when it finally found its way up the tower steps to Vita's study, was a fat one, full of photographs and newspaper clippings, besides Andrew's usual newsy letter, with his odd bits of information and requests for some from Vita. She in turn found it necessary to answer him in lists. It seemed the best way to impart as much news as possible on two small sheets of paper.

February 10, 1953

My dear friend Andrew

Your letter arrived this morning and gave me great pleasure. I liked seeing the photographs of your house, garden, and companion. (*blot* Oh dear!) I was amused also by the bits about Harold; Bodiam Castle is a wonderful place; it was built in 1380 by an ancestor of mine; Lord Curzon bought it, and gave it to the nation. How inaccurate the Press always is: Harold was never Lord Curzon's private secretary; he just worked in the Foreign Office

Feb. 10. 1953

Sissinghurst Castle,
Kent.

My dear friend Andrew
           Your letter arrived this morning
and gave me great pleasure. I liked seeing
the photographs of your house, garden, and
companion. (● Oh dear!) I was amused
also by the bits about Harold; Bodiam
Castle is a wonderful place; it was built
in 1380 by an ancestor of mine; Lord Curzon
bought it, and gave it to the nation.
How inaccurate the Press always is: Harold
was never Lord Curzon's private secretary;
he just worked in the Foreign Office
when Lord Curzon was Secretary of State for
foreign affairs. He didn't want to
accept the K.C.V.O, he didn't want in
the least to become Sir Harold, but as
the Manchester Guardian rightly remarks
it is a personal gift of the Sovereign and
he couldn't refuse when the Queen insisted.

Page one of Vita's letter of February 10, 1953.

when Lord Curzon was Secretary of State for foreign affairs. He didn't want to accept the K.C.V.O., he didn't
want in the least to become Sir Harold, but as the Manchester Guardian rightly remarks it is a personal gift of the
Sovereign and he couldn't refuse when the Queen insisted. I think he would rather have been made a Companion of Honour,—as I am.

The Vestal Virgin—she's by a Serbian sculptor called
Rosandic.

It will be lovely to have some more Andrew Zinnias,
whether they arrive on St. Valentine's day or not. They
will make up for the horrible winter we have had, starting
in November and culminating now in appalling floods,
both here and in Holland. Thank you so much; you *are*
kind.

No chance of your coming over for the Coronation, I
suppose? I shall see the procession I hope, as Harold's club
is on the route and he has drawn two tickets in the ballot. I
should dearly like to show you Sissinghurst.

> Ever affectionately
> Vita

Andrew by now considered it a matter of pride to time the
sending of the year's gift of the peppermint-stick zinnia seeds to
arrive at Sissinghurst on Valentine's Day. However, weeks went
by without any acknowledgment of their arrival from Vita, so
Andrew sent off a letter to inquire about the fate of the precious
seed. By that time he had obtained the novel *The Easter Party*
and had read it with his usual admiration for Vita's work. Andrew inclined toward matters religious, even mystical, and
Vita's novel, full of Christian and pagan imagery, greatly ap

pealed to him. Vita's letter to protest her innocence of forgetting to mention the arrival of the seeds also referred to her novel.

April 1, 1953

But Andrew, dear unknown Andrew, I wrote *at once* to tell you the zinnia seed had arrived just right for St. Valentine's Day. I can hope only that our letters have crossed each other on the ocean, and that you are now re-assured about the safe arrival of your packet. I haven't sown them yet; we have to wait till the middle of May.

I can't think what you will have made of The Easter Party—you probably hated it. Very few reviewers seem to have understood it at all, though I must say I have seen some very intelligent notices from American critics. Most people seem to have been completely puzzled by it.

I do like the idea of your St. Francis Shrine—and wish I could see it. Yes, I promise you faithfully that if ever I cross the Atlantic again I will let you know and will invite myself boldly to Windslip. What fun that would be.

Now do write and tell me you got my other letter, thanking you for the huge packet of Andrew zinnias.

Your friend,
Vita

At the end of May, a busy time for a gardener and an especially busy time for Vita this year, she took a moment to send off a short letter to Andrew, accompanying it with some seeds of the Scarlet Pimpernel plant. Despite all Andrew's efforts to nurture them, they were not able to grow in the soil of the rocky Maine coast.

ACQUAINTANCESHIP

May 29, 1953

My dear friend Andrew

All the Andrew zinnias are sown and coming up finely, so here is the Scarlet Pimpernel as a present from them.

My garden is having a lot of American visitors. We had a coach load of members of the American Men's Garden Club here the other day. Why were you not with them?

The Coronation has brought many Americans, and I hope everything will go off with due pageantry to please everybody. I am going to see the procession from Harold's club—and we also go to an evening party at Buckingham Palace, which should be a beautiful sight.

The garden is a blaze of flowers just now, how I wish you could see it. Roses coming out everywhere and smelling to Heaven.

My younger son is getting married in July, to a very charming and pretty girl called Philippa Tennyson d'Eyncourt. So I am pleased about that. He is the one who is in the House of Commons: Nigel. They are coming down to stay here today so I must go and put some flowers in their rooms. This means that I must take my leave of you, which I do with regret. Bless you, and let me hear sometime again from you, won't you?

Yours
Vita

Nigel Nicolson had phoned his parents about his engagement on March 30. The wedding took place on July 30 at St. Margaret's, Westminster. Harold Nicolson recorded the occasion in his diary:

There is an awning and a large crowd. Philippa arrives on the dot, and then the lovely ceremony begins. Afterwards we drive off to Fishmonger's Hall. Everything there is magnificent, and V. and I stand beside the Tennyson-d'Eyncourts shaking hands with troops of people. Ben makes a sweet little speech, and then Niggs replies, referring to our happily married life and love for each other. This brings a lump to my throat and tears to V.'s eyes.[5]

Both the Nicolsons were delighted with their beautiful new daughter-in-law and looked forward to the arrival of grandchildren. Philippa was to provide much pleasure and companionship for all of the Nicolsons. Six years after Vita's death, she would publish a selection of Vita's *Observer* articles under the title V. *Sackville-West's Garden Book*.

The private festivities of the Nicolson family were accompanied on the largest imaginable scale by the nationwide celebrations for the coronation of Queen Elizabeth II. The then Princess Elizabeth had been traveling with her husband, Philip, in Kenya when her father, the king, had died the previous year. As Harold Nicolson put it, "She became Queen while perched in a tree in Africa, watching the rhinoceros come down to the pool to drink."[6] The coronation took place on June 2, 1953. Vita and Harold Nicolson saw the ceremony on a television set at the Travellers Club. They then watched the procession from places in a stand along the route from the abbey. Vita's next letter told Andrew of her impressions.

Oh, we've been having such festivities here. Really *so* beautiful. I hope you saw the television film in the Abbey. Harold and I went to an evening party at Buckingham Palace; it was like the old days, everybody blazing with jewels and uniforms and decorations.—scarlet Lifeguardsmen standing about, and all the Palace servants in their gold State liveries instead of the battle-dress they used to wear, and the Queen looking so young and far prettier than she does in photographs. London has gone absolutely mad and so has the country: there isn't the smallest cottage, however remote, that isn't fluttering with flags. It is really rather touching.

Vita in fact was so moved by the events that she wrote a poem about the coronation. Her offering to the young queen on the threshold of an arduous yet thrilling career, it was printed in the *Times Literary Supplement* for June 5.

JUNE 2ND, 1953 [7]

Madam, how strange to be your Majesty
How strange to wake in an ordinary bed
And, half awake, to think "Now who am I?"
As we all think to ourselves when with the dawn
The birds first rouse us with the rising sun
And we recall the little facts of our lives,
The engagements we have that day, the photographs
Framed on the table, the books, the telephone,
And piece the bits of our life together, the worries,
    the obligations,
Eventually making, as the cloud of sleep
Disperses, a quick report renewed of our daily self
And of who we are and of what we have to do.

Am I Elizabeth or Lilibet?
Are the Great Officers of State preparing?
Are Charles and Anne asleep in the nursery?

The main purpose of Vita's letter of June 14 was not, however, to describe the coronation to Andrew but to alert him to a radio broadcast that she had just completed recording.

> This is just to say that I have been recording a short talk for the North American service, in a series called "This I Believe." The BBC could not tell me when it would be transmitted, but apparently it is quite a well known series and is produced by Ed Murrow, I think they said, daily. Perhaps it would amuse you to listen? I am sorry not to be able to be more precise, and apparently you don't have a Radio Times, as we have, giving the daily programmes for a week at a time (Because you have so many networks and we have only the BBC) so it means looking in the newspaper every morning.

The indefatigable Andrew immediately fired off a letter to the radio series itself. A courteous reply from the "This I Believe" series informed him that the program had not yet been scheduled for the United States. He was not to hear the broadcast until the following April. Vita's short essay on faith very clearly shows the progress of her thought from an early interest in Catholicism through to the eclectic ideas of *The Easter Party*.

THIS I BELIEVE . . .
THE THOUGHT THAT MAN IS A SPECK OF DUST
GIVES SENSE OF PROPORTION, SAYS AUTHOR

English novelist Vita Sackville-West whose father was a distinguished Lord and whose grandmother was a famous gypsy dancer,

ACQUAINTANCESHIP

reveals her personal creed. This is one of a series of statements by thinking, useful people in all walks of life, and is presented by Edward R. Murrow.

By Vita Sackville-West
English Novelist

My religion, if I have one, is of the profoundest humility. It can be resolved into the few words: I simply do not know. Who am I to pretend to know? I am less than a speck of dust on a speck of a satellite revolving around a speck of a star which we on earth are pleased to call the Sun, but which in fact is only an insignificant member of one galaxy in a universe which we know to contain a million of other galaxies of equal size, whose origin is obscure to us, but whose date is supposed by present-day scientists to go back to four billion years.

These figures give me a sense of proportion, quite different from the comforting creed of the Christian church, which tells me that I am all-important to a Creator who cares for me individually with loving-kindness and mercy. I am quite prepared to believe in something which we, conveniently, call God; but thereby I mean something inexplicable and incomprehensible to our human minds. Something which I would prefer to call X; or the Originating Force; or the Mathematical Mind; or what you will. That there is a Something behind the creation—an Absolute Abstract, if you like, to which in our human dread and weakness we must give a personal name, and to which we must attach such human attributes as mercy and justice and loving-kindness, for which Nature shows us no justification at all—I can have no doubt whatsoever: it is an inescapable conviction. My only quarrel is with man's interpretation of these mysteries—that is, the interpretation of the great organization of the churches—and in particular with the theory of man's redemption through Christ. The beautiful figure of Christ appears to

(43)

me as a necessary device to soften our terror of the unknown Creator; a gentle link, a semi-human advocate.

I believe in what we call goodness, or essential and ultimate perfection. This raises the great problem of evil. Is there any such thing, as regards the universe at large, or does it merely affect the life on our small planet, in the imperfection of mankind and the apparent cruelty of Nature? I like to believe so, but this again must take its place among the unresolvable mysteries. It seems to me, however, that there can be no room for any fundamental blemish in a creation of such unimaginable magnitude and invention.

I believe that, in the last resort, that everything is of a piece and that the gigantic pattern could be seen, had we but the vision and the knowledge to perceive it. I believe that there exists no necessary discrepancy between science and religion, but I must insist again that by "religion" I do not here mean our human theology, but a far greater and humbler faith in an ultimate wisdom.

Despite the importance of her subject to Andrew, he was perhaps even more enchanted to hear Vita's speaking voice. She responded to his excited letter, "How very odd it seems! All those miles away . . . to be in your room talking to you."[8]

Vita's autumn of 1953 seems to have been dominated even more than usual by gardening concerns. In August she and Harold had driven through Scotland, where they saw many famous gardens. They also visited their favorite English garden, Hidcote in Gloucestershire. On their return to Sissinghurst, Harold loyally remarked, "The garden is looking well, and we prefer it to all those we have seen, with the exception of Hidcote."[9] In all seasons, Sissinghurst was a place of beauty. Vita wrote to Andrew in October:

The Andrew zinnias have been such a success this summer, and are still flowering, though threatened by frost now. The little Persian carpet ones are still particularly good, and I have a bunch on my table in front of me as I write to you—I picked them this evening to bring indoors, in case the first frost of the year caught them during the night, and I might find them all blackened when I came down in the morning.

Our Autumn colouring is quite good, though I know it can't compare with the famous colouring of Maine and Vermont. I plant things in my garden especially for autumn colour, you see, because we have not the wonderful colouring in the woods which you get—so one has to do one's best with little cherry trees and some other red-and-yellow-and-pink trees which are really very lovely just now.

Do you think you will ever come to see Sissinghurst? A friend of mine, a journalist, rang me up suddenly; I thought she was in New York; but she said "Oh, it's only 12 hours flight, so I've come across for a couple of days to London—I'm going back tomorrow."

Well, . . . if it's as easy as all that? . . . But perhaps you don't like flying. I hate it myself, and nothing would induce me. But then I am old-fashioned, and perhaps you are too.

There was no Christmas letter from Vita that year. But on January 3, 1954, she wrote: "Thank goodness Christmas is over—we managed to be fairly quiet, but our neighbors *will* give cocktail parties, which we both loathe but are more or less obliged to attend once a year." Harold had already voiced similar sentiments in a letter to his daughter-in-law. "There is one thing that I feel we lack as a family, and that is social gaiety. . . . The result is that we do not enjoy cocktail parties and make such an effort not to show our displeasure that we become taut, strained, dehydrated, absurd and unreal. Now the one thing we are not is unreal. So I hate Christmas, and I wish David's royal city were not celebrated in vermouth and gin."[10]

Andrew had complained to Vita that he was unable to obtain a volume of her poetry. She wrote in her January 3 letter: "I was horrified to learn that you had wanted to get hold of my poems and failed; I don't think I have ever published a book of verse in America, but I will send you some. Meanwhile I have obeyed your behest and written out a little poem I thought you might like." The poem was "Evening."[11]

> When little lights in little ports come out,
> Quivering down through water with the stars,
> And all the fishing fleet of slender spars
> Range at their moorings, veer with tide about;
>
> When race of wind is still and sails are furled,
> And underneath our single riding-light
> The curve of black-ribbed deck gleams palely white,
> And slumbrous waters pool a slumbrous world,
>
> —Then, and then only, have I thought how sweet
> Old age might sink upon a windy youth,
> Quiet beneath the riding-light of truth,
> Weathered through storms, and gracious in retreat.

The letter itself ended, "Is it too late to wish you a Happy New Year? Anyhow I can wish you a happy 1954. I do hope it will be."

Vita's next letter to "My dear friend Andrew" was dated February 14.

We have had a frightful spell of frost and snow, after a very mild January, and I fear it will have done a lot of

Evening.

When little lights in little ports come out,
Quivering down through water with the stars,
And all the fishing fleet of slender spars
Range at their moorings, veer with tide about;

When race of wind is stilled and sails are furled,
And underneath our single riding-light
The curve of black-ribbed deck gleams palely white,
And slumbrous waters pool a slumbrous world,

— Then, and then only, have I thought how sweet
Old age might sink upon a windy youth,
Quiet beneath the riding-light of truth,
Weathered through storms, and gracious in retreat.

The copy of the poem "Evening," which Vita sent to Andrew.

damage in the garden, accompanied as it was by bitter winds. It is mild again now, and things are beginning to grow—several little spring flowers are blooming—and today is St. Valentine when the birds are supposed to start nesting.

I hope you are happy and well, and looking forward to the Spring. I am!

Andrew had inquired if he might add some other varieties of zinnia to the packet of "Andrew zinnias" he mailed to Vita each spring. "Blaze sounds lovely, and as I have an orange-red garden it would be perfect. I like any of the Burpee ones,—Persian carpet or Fantasy, for instance. *Not* white, since I can get those here," she replied.

On April 3, she wrote:

Andrew dear, the lovely packet of zinnia seeds has just arrived, and I write instantly to thank you. You are more than kind. Also, the photograph of Windslip in the snow—which nearly gave me a cold in the head merely to look at it. I hope you have emerged from under that white blanket by now. We are still pretty chilly here, but not so bad as all that.

The garden is beginning to show colour, and the orchard is full of daffodils— Do you have daffodils in America? Also our carpet of coloured primroses and polyanthus is looking nice; I have some of the fine Californian strain amongst them. I must send you a postcard of them.

Lots of spring flowering bulbs are also in bloom, scillas, hyacinths, chionodoxas, jonquils, and masses of

anemones—and some early flowering cherries. In fact it is all looking quite gay, but we get cloudy days and long for the sun to come out. My mother always used to say that the sun was the greatest of all painters.

Well I must stop I suppose, but not without sending you my love and my really grateful thanks,

Vita

The same April 3 post brought Andrew the promised post-card of primroses "blue, pink, red, yellow, white, orange, buff," "growing under nut trees."

Later the same month, Andrew learned that his close friend Ann Merriam was planning a trip to England during the summer. Ann was the mother of young Tom Merriam, who had occasioned the opening of Andrew's correspondence with Vita.

(49)

The postcard of the primroses, April 13, 1954. *Courtesy of Tempo Labs.*

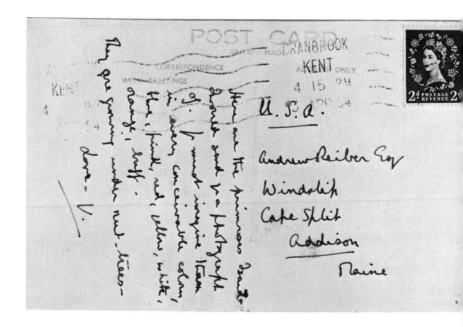

One of Andrew's greatest delights was to introduce his cherished friends to one another. He enjoyed "mixing" people, and believed, to use his own metaphor, that the best cocktail in the world was the "cocktail homo sapiens." In the spring of 1954 Andrew was thrilled at the thought of his beloved Ann and his unknown friend Vita meeting and enjoying each other's company, and he wrote Vita immediately to ask if Ann might visit Sissinghurst. Vita replied on April 25:

Of course I shall be *delighted* to see her here, so please tell her to let me know the date as soon as she knows it herself. . . . It will be the greatest pleasure to meet a friend of yours, and I only wish it were you yourself.

. . . .

One thing I regret is that the garden here is quite at its worst in July; the roses will be over, and your friend will be disappointed. Never mind, it can't be helped.

. . . .

We're still horribly cold here—but the spring flowers are lovely, the daffodils [in] blossom, and anemones.

Preparations for Ann's trip went forward. Andrew was perhaps more excited than Ann herself. In early June came a brief note from Vita.

4th June 1954

My dear Andrew,

Please forgive a typewritten letter for once, but it is just to say that I got your letter announcing the arrival of Mrs.

Merriam. I shall be so pleased to welcome her here, but can you give me her address in England as she will not be able to get me on the telephone unless I give it to her. We keep it out of the telephone directory. I will of course write again to you when I have seen her. I am not going to France until August so there will be plenty of time.

Yours affectionately,
Vita

Andrew heard no more of his scheme until late July, when he received a postcard of the Herb Garden at Sissinghurst with two scribbled messages on the reverse side. The first read, "Can you believe it—here I am at Sissinghurst—a most beautiful and memorable day. I'll write you, Ann." The second was: "We wish you were here with us, Vita."

True to her promise, Ann sat down in her hotel in the nearby town of Sevenoaks the very next day and wrote Andrew a four-page letter detailing her visit.

The Ormiston Country Hotel
Sevenoaks-Kent-July 21st, 1954

Dear old Pixie:—

The great day has come and gone,—and sometime you will get a card (regular mail) signed by both Vita and Ann in the garden of Sissinghurst— The good fairies were with me for never did a lovelier day dawn in England than yesterday. I was invited for one o'clock and on the dot I climbed out of the car. (Yes, darling—so as not to disgrace you, I hired a car to get me there—Nearly 3 £'s!) I was shown into the garden and there I met your Vita.

I can't describe both her and her surroundings—You

The postcard sent to Andrew jointly by Vita and Ann—the herb garden at Sissinghurst. *Courtesy of E. A. Sweetman and Son, Ltd.*

know long-winded me—I'd never finish—Having to choose, I think I'll go on about her and leave the description of her surroundings until I see you. I'll simply say that her garden was indescribably lovely seen under the soft bright sunshine—and the English do have an insurmountable advantage over us in their backgrounds of old walls, old masonry—not to mention old moats supporting a swan or two—

As for Vita—first I'll try to tell you how she looks —She's as tall as I am, possibly taller (she doesn't stand too straight) and I should say her frame was larger, though there isn't an extra pound on it—Her hair at one time must have been golden, but it is now short, drab and uncared for—Her eyes are blue and rather prominent, her complexion ruddy—In her youth she must have been handsome, perhaps beautiful—but alas you know what time does to us all. (I expect she is in her early sixties.) I don't think I ever met a woman who cared less. She was dressed in a mustard colored blouse, brown skirt and dark red corduroy jacket. I might say that she was absolutely oblivious to her personal appearance, if it hadn't been for the fact that from time to time she pulled out an orange (poisonous color to me) lipstick and did her lips—She smokes as much as you do, Andrew, and the only touch of luxury about her was a thin Gold cigarette case. But she was kindness and cordiality itself—Her voice is low and her manner self-contained, but she made me feel welcome at once. There was no awkwardness—She began asking about you and seemed genuinely interested in all I had to tell her. She asked me what you looked like but before I could begin, she stopped me. "No," she said—"Let me tell you first what I *think* he looks like." I don't know whether her description will irritate, amuse or mystify you. If she had seen the Squire [12] she couldn't have described him better—tall, spare, distinguished with dark eyes and iron grey hair—in his seventies—Of course I had to tell her she was wrong and then tried to make her see you as well as I could through my eyes. In the end she wasn't disappointed.

You remember when we were talking things over at Windslip the Squire began chaffing us about what I was going to tell Vita about you, and I said I thought you should have confidence in the bonds of friendship—So you may—I don't think you need have any regrets over the

Vita's desk in 1951. *Courtesy of the* Illustrated London News.

personality I presented to Vita nor the impact it had on her. I tried to give her a true and living picture of you, just as I'm trying to give you a true and living picture of her. If I said she was simply wonderful, everything she said was simply wonderful and every move she made was simply wonderful,—the picture would be meaningless.

After luncheon we went up to her study in the tower. (You've seen pictures of it—she says she's sent you all her post cards) and there we talked about books and authors—I immediately espied a photograph of the portrait of the Brontë sisters in the National Gallery, and discovered she is as enthusiastic—or rather, values the personality of Emily Brontë as much as I always have. She strongly urged me to go to Yorkshire and have a look at Emily's moors—which I've had in mind all along. . . .

I asked her about her own writing, but on this subject she was rather uncommunicative, so naturally I didn't pursue it. She did say, however, that she is working on a biography and that shortly she is going to the south of France in search of material. I wonder if it is in pursuit of one of her strange Spanish forebears—Which reminds me (I ought to keep it as a surprise but here I go and spoil it) I'm bringing you home a copy of "Pepita" with a nice little foreword in Vita's own hand.[13]

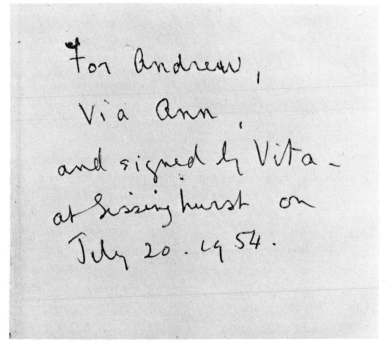

The inscription in Andrew's copy of *Pepita*.

. . . .

Give my love to the Squire and keep all you want for
yourself. It won't be too long before I see you and then I'll
tell you everything I haven't written.

Devotedly,
Ann

The little chintz-covered cushion stuffed with pine needles
from the Maine woods that Andrew had entrusted to Ann to
carry brought Vita much pleasure. The object is a traditional
present, as it bears the scent of the Maine pines, but this particular one was special, since Andrew had carefully chosen a
puzzle print composed of profiles of Victoria and Albert that he
was certain would amuse Vita. Her graceful note of thanks did
not come, however, until October.

Oct. 1, 1954
My dear Andrew, dear friend Andrew,

So many things seem to have been happening, —such a
lot of people, and going abroad, etc.—that I simply cannot
remember if I ever wrote to you after your very nice Ann's
visit here. I know I meant to, and then I thought of you
again when I heard of a hurricane ravaging the coast of
Maine, but whether the letter ever got written I just can't
be sure. Forgive me?

I did enjoy the day with Ann. I know she will have told
you about it, in fact you wrote and told me she had. And
you got our postcard. I liked her so much, and felt that we
were in harmony—I hope I was right.

Your fir-tip pillow is the greatest joy to me. Not only
does it smell heavenly but it is just the perfect thing for a

Vita's 1954 Christmas card, the entrance to the tower. *Courtesy of E. A.*
Sweetman and Son, Ltd.

person who reads in bed, as I do. One's ordinary pillows are too soft, and yours provides the "prop" at the back of one's neck. I really love it, including the Victoria and Albert chintz. At first, I could not think what the good smell reminded me of: warm pine woods, of course.

My son Nigel and his wife flew to New York last night, as he had been invited to lecture at Harvard.[14] He has never been to America before and was very thrilled about it. They will only be there a fortnight, as he is in the House of Commons and Parliament will be re-assembling. I hate politics myself, but he loves them, which I suppose is a good thing in a young man. Lucky somebody likes them!

Now with my love and thank you again for my lovely pillow, which really *is* a treasure.

Vita

The Nicolsons had spent much of August motoring in France. Besides the Lascaux caves with their famous wall paintings, they visited Montaigne's tower and George Sand's house at Nohant.

The little pillow was mentioned again on Vita's Christmas postcard to Andrew, this time a picture of the entrance to the tower: "This is just to bring my love and good wishes for Christmas from my pink tower to your snowy Maine, and to say that the pine needle pillow never seems to lose its delicious scent. . . . I hope you have the sort of Christmas you like —and a happy year in 1955—from Vita."

Friendship

1955–1960

By 1955 Vita and Andrew's relationship had solidified. Months might go by without an exchange of letters, but that did not mean that their long-distance friendship had diminished. The mysterious bond that evidenced itself in the very first few notes had revealed itself to be caused by common interests—gardening, books, dogs. Andrew had already exhibited his uncanny ability to select just the right modest little gift to flatter and delight Vita. He was quick to pick up any hint of her wishes, be it for plants, people, or pine pillows. She certainly appreciated his attentions and was touched by such thoughtfulness from an unknown person. The romance of Andrew's faraway life in Maine intrigued her, and she enjoyed contrasting her life with his. Her letter of February 17, 1955, refers to many facets of their friendship.

FRIENDSHIP

My dear Andrew

So long since I have written to you! I got your precious Valentine of zinnias on just the right day. Can't plant Them yet: too cold. I am saving them up till April. And then I got the glass-flower leaflet,—all from you, and your kind thought of me constantly—and the Pine-pillow which is my joy every night. I put it behind my head, and read my book, and delicious wafts of pine-scent come to me each time I move, and I think "Dear unknown Andrew!"

Really, that little pine-pillow is quite the nicest thing I ever had. It is a true treasure, and I hope its scent never fades.

I lead such a funny mixed life. Shall I give you a cross-section of it? This morning I sat on the Bench—do you know what that is? It means I am a Magistrate, or what we call a Justice of the Peace—and I have to be all tidy in a coat-and-skirt and a hat—and have to administer justice to my fellow countrymen. Then I come home and change into my old gardening clothes, which means breeches and high boots, and I go and tramp about in mud and snow. Then as dusk falls I come in, and write the book I am trying to write—and then I really feel *myself*—in my tower, shut away. I become an author again, and am happy. But that is not the whole story. Another side of my life suddenly barges in. The telephone rings. Will I lunch with the Queen tomorrow, to meet the Shah of Persia?

Well . . . one can't refuse. It amounts to a Royal Command. Besides, it will amuse me, much as I hate going to London.

So there you are, Andrew, you see what a curiously mixed life I lead, and what a queer person you have got yourself attached to.

V.

It was fitting that the Nicolsons should be included at a royal luncheon party during the state visit of the Shah of Persia (Iran). Not only had Harold Nicolson been born in Teheran, but he had also held the post of Counsellor at the British Embassy from 1925 to 1927. Vita had joined him in Iran for two long visits, resulting directly in her travel books *Passenger to Teheran* and *Twelve Days* and indirectly in her famous poem of Kent, *The Land*. Both Vita and Harold felt strong ties to Iran and loved its country and its people, so different from the English, yet in a peculiar way complementary. Harold reported the luncheon party in his diary:

> Viti and I go to Buckingham Palace for a luncheon for the Shah. In come Winston[15] and Clemmie, looking grand. Then the Iranian Ambassador. Then the Queen Mother. Then the Queen and the Duke. And finally the Shah and his wife. Viti sits between Sir Ivone Kirkpatrick and Winston. The latter is in his best mood and talks gaily to her about history.[16]

The spring of 1955 was a time of illness for both the Nicolsons. Harold suffered from a bad attack of sciatica and then experienced two slight strokes. Vita injured her back. Harold told Philippa of her accident, which occurred at the end of March:

> Vita was going down her turret staircase when she lost her balance. Owing to the weakness of her back muscles,

which in turn is due to arthritis, she could not recover herself, and to prevent herself falling downstairs, she sat down abruptly on the step. This gave her a frightful bruise and terrific pain in getting up or sitting down. I was afraid she had broken something. She refused to go to bed or see a doctor (she always does), and she limped about all yesterday in real agony.[17]

When Vita did consent to seek medical attention, an X-ray showed that she had cracked the sacrum in her back. The healing process was slow and made more so by her refusal to remain in bed. On May 13 she wrote Andrew:

I am still rather crippled. I forget if I told you that I had fallen on some brick steps and cracked a bone in my back. It is getting rapidly better, but I still can't stoop, which is infuriating for a gardener. Can't pick a flower, or plant a seedling, or pull up a weed! Anyhow I can walk about, and that is much to be thankful for.

By summertime the health and temperament of both Nicolsons were much improved. They were excited about the wedding of their elder son, Benedict, to Luisa Vertova, an Italian who had been working for the art critic Bernard Berenson in Florence. Then, too, Vita had just acquired a second-hand Jaguar, a car that she had coveted for some time. Harold Nicolson remarked of the purchase, "Viti has bought her Jaguar, which is an insane thing to have done, but wise."[18] This cheerful note is apparent in her next letter to Andrew. Her usual white writing paper with the red inscription "V. Sackville-West, Sissinghurst Castle, Kent" had given way to a new blue air-letter form.

DEAREST ANDREW

July 31, 1955

My dear Andrew. Look, I have acquired some lovely blue airmail paper, on purpose for you. I know I've been awfully bad about writing, but in summer the days go past like jet aeroplanes and I never seem to get a minute to myself. Now I am on the eve of going to Florence for a week; I think I told you my son Benedict was engaged to a Florentine girl, and we are going out for the wedding. It will be very hot! I shall take a large straw hat and my Spanish fan. Then in October we shall go to France for a fortnight. Did I tell you I had a new car, a Jaguar? It is very powerful, and I am secretly terrified of it, but French roads are very different from our narrow twisty Kentish lanes.

The garden has really been lovely this summer: roses have flowered as never before, and now they have been succeeded by masses of white lilies. It won't last much longer, for August is always a bad month here. It gets nicer again in September and October. We are suffering from a prolonged drought and have to water, which is never quite the same as rain. I wish I could see your autumn colours.

I don't know if you've ever heard Ruth Draper in her sketch 'Showing the garden.' If so, you will understand my feelings when she came here the other day. What an artist she is—and so nice.

Your zinnias are looking grand. They are all along the foot of a wall with Morning Glory clambering behind them. Very showy indeed. You know Morning Glory of course? The Heavenly Blue convolvulus.

Now do send me a line which I shall find here on my

return from Italy, and tell me if you are well. Oh, my back: it has quite recovered, but it took about four months, and was I cross.

With love,
Vita

Now that their correspondence was all of five years old, Andrew felt he might take exception to what he considered the formal way in which Vita opened her letters to him. However affectionate her closings, Vita usually began in what Andrew thought to be the manner of a bank manager addressing an overdrawn customer. His complaint generated a playful reply:

September 22, 1955

My dear Andrew. No, I am given to understand that the American and the English habit is reversed. To us, *My dear* is a far warmer form than just *Dear*, yet if I put just Dear Andrew it looks so cold and formal to my English eyes. And if my American publisher begins his letter to me *My* dear it looks very personal and intimate! so what is one to do? I shall take refuge in *Dearest Andrew* which is what we reserve for our real friends.

"Dearest Andrew," therefore, I begin all over again.

. . . .

And now this morning I get your letter with amusing enclosures, especially the one about the little Persian train. Harold and I and Gladwyn Jebb, who was then a young secretary in our legation in Teheran, nearly got run down by that train once. Our car stuck on the level crossing, and we saw the train advancing towards us at its maximum speed of 30 miles an hour. We cleared it just in time, but it would have been pretty ironical to get smashed up by a train in a country where there was then only one train and one railway track eight miles long.

So you see that your enclosure was particularly well chosen, and took me back over many years.

. . . .

Harold and I are off to France for a fortnight on October 6th. We are going to the South-west (Dordogne), and then to Provence.

—Oh, here I must interrupt my letter to say that six white pigeons are cooing to me on the ledges of my tower just outside my window. Such a soft summer sound! They walk up and down the ledge, and sometimes come into my room. I don't encourage this idea, as they knock things over and are not house-trained, but I do love them.

This is a rather scrambly letter, but I write as it comes.

And oh! Andrew! you wouldn't send me a refill of pine needles for the Queen Victoria-Prince Consort pillow, would you? That pillow had been my joy for months, and the scent is now fading. It was the nicest thing I ever had and I couldn't replace it from any shop,—only you can replace,—and I could *refill* Queen Victoria and Prince Albert. If I could get pine needles from Maine I wouldn't bother you, but obviously I can't, so I have to beg.

Your Beggar,

V.

Andrew was of course thrilled by his beggar's request for the refill of pine needles. Rather than simply send the needles, he had a whole new pillow made up, again searching for an unusual fabric to please Vita. Once more he was successful.

Nov. 4, 1955

Andrew, the parcel has arrived! I was getting worried about it, because you wrote so long ago to say it had been dispatched, even before I went off to France—and then when I came back from France, it wasn't here. So I was afraid it might have got lost on the way, but this morning it came and smells delicious, Arcadian sheet and all, to remind me of the colours of sunrise at Tezd-i-Khast (oh, how far away!) and also to suggest the kindness of dear unknown Andrew, also so far away.

. . . .

Our jaunt to France was a great success. We had perfect summer weather and saw much lovely country and many

lovely things. . . . We avoided large towns and smart re-
sorts, and just wandered about the side-roads in the Dordogne and Provence, looking at the country and finding
our way up into remote hill-villages, as far off the beaten
track as we could get.

It was fun. The Jaguar adored the long straight roads, on
the way there and back.

What would you like me to send you for Christmas?
One will have to begin thinking about Christmas before
long—especially for parcels to America. See how long the
pillow took to come! So please tell me—and meanwhile
thank you again, dear Andrew, for the redolent pine-
pillow and for your friendship.

V.

Andrew's next gift was equally unique and equally appreciated. He prevailed on a friend to take Vita a box of Pepitas,
Mexican pine nuts. Vita wrote, "They really are delicious, and
something I have never met before. . . . It is so amusing their
having my grandmother's name." Her Christmas present to Andrew was his favorite tobacco mixture from Dunhills. She re-
gretted the delay in his receiving it in her first letter of 1956.

February 6, 1956

Dearest Andrew

Your Valentine has preceded its date, but not its welcome. The packet of zinnia seeds arrived just at the right
moment to make me think of summer when snow lay in-
ches deep on the ground and all our water-pipes froze as
they always do the moment the thermometer drops in En-

gland. (Our plumbing system is truly mediaeval and would you believe it, they go on building *new* houses and cottages just the same, with the pipes on the *outside* walls. Then the thaw comes, and there are floods of water all over the rooms. We must be mad.)

Anyway, there is the huge generous packet on my table; I shake it, and it rattles, and I know that *every seed means a flower.* I can hope only that my own little packet for you has reached its destination by now; I did tell you, didn't I, that *Dunhill* warned me it would be very slow? But you must get your pipe-dreams sooner or later.

You wrote me such a very dear letter on January 15. I have just been stuck here all the time, which I like, and don't propose to go near London even for the day until the end of the month. I must go then, because much to my astonishment I have been awarded a Gold Medal by the Royal Horticultural Society. Have I already boasted to you about this? I expect I have, because I was rather pleased, but I was even more surprised than pleased as it generally goes to old gentlemen of over 80, who have devoted the whole of their lives to horticulture.

Now that's quite enough about me.

Oh, but I must tell you that today I received an enormous box of flowers by air from the French Riviera —carnations, hyacinths, and God knows what, all fresh and scented. My room looks like a florist's shop, and smells like a scent-shop,—or perhaps I ought to compare it to a prima donna's dressing room?

I send you my love and more thanks for the zinnias and all your kindness to your unknown.

V.

DEAREST ANDREW

Despite her rather offhand reference to the honor bestowed on her by the Royal Horticultural Society, Vita was clearly touched by it. She knew that in this case she was receiving recognition for a real and precious achievement, and such recognition was sweet. She gave Andrew more news of it in her next letter, written on March 7.

You asked about my medal. Very pretty—and *real* gold I would have you know—none of your alloys or synthetic substitutes. We still do this sort of thing with some *chic* in this poor old country. I felt rather like a school-child, going up to the rostrum to receive my prize from the President of the Royal Horticultural Society,[19] who has almost as much charm as his sister (the Queen Mother,) and is a friend of mine anyway so we winked at each other across the table as he made me a solemn little speech.

Most of this letter was concerned with Vita's winter garden, but it also expressed her pleasure at Andrew's latest surprise. He had discovered her birthday, which was March 9, and dispatched a special card to send best wishes.

My dear Andrew, You really are clever, fancy discovering the date of my birthday in a cottage in Maine, and managing to get a greeting to me just in time! Wonderful. It gave me great pleasure.

We have emerged from the snow—but I fear we have many garden casualties. I daren't look too closely. The spring things have shot up in an amazing way since the snow went and we had a few days of sun: there are lots of crocuses full of bees, grape hyacinths, scillas, chionodoxa; and the chorus of birds in the morning has become an orchestra.

FRIENDSHIP

I wonder how long your winter is? Do you have snow and frost regularly from November to March, or what? Here, we had soft mild weather up to the end of January, and then February came in like a sort of steel trap closing on us, but now it is quite spring-like although of course we may still get snow, frost, and wind from the north and east, only one knows it won't be so severe or last so long.

And we are never prepared for cold weather. You can almost hear a sort of machine-gun of bursting pipes all over the country.

. . . .

I must write an article for the Observer. It is extraordinary how quickly the weeks roll round, like a prayer wheel: no sooner do I think I have cleared the beastly thing off than I realise it is time to start another one.

I shall write about the little things of spring, but before I start doing that I must thank you once more dear Andrew for your birthday letter and your good wishes.

from Vita

Andrew had to wait several months for another letter from Vita. It came full of apologies, as well as the usual news of the garden.

August 2, 1956

My dear Andrew,

I feel it is ages and ages since I have written to you—I simply don't know how the days slide away, and all the things I mean to do never get done, or else something happens to interrupt my intentions.

You must lead a much quieter life than I. In the summer months, I get invaded by people, and lose my head sometimes with all the things I have to do and people to see. Into the midst of this, I try to look after my garden, almost a whole-time job.

Anyhow, I do think of you constantly and try to imagine the very different life you lead.

I have been re-reading your last letter, June 1st. Did I ever meet Emmuska Orczy, you ask? Yes, I did. She was a vast woman, so kindly and motherly to me, her very young fan. I couldn't have realised, at that age, what a nuisance I was being: but she could not have been kinder or more welcoming.

Now what else can I tell you? The Andrew zinnias are coming up, and just starting into flower. We had an awful gale last week, which wrecked trees and plants, but the Andrew zinnias didn't suffer. The garden looked like a battle-field, strewn with damage, —huge branches blown down, and everything turned inside out; unripe apples all over the orchard on the ground; magnolias smashed in half; tiles flying off the roofs; and my dog propelled at a run across the lawn because he couldn't keep his feet.

We don't bargain for this sort of hurricane in July—not in this island of ours. You deal with far more violent extremes in your U.S.A.

Well, dear Andrew, this comes with my love although rather belated,

Vita

Another letter followed hard on the heels of that one, for Andrew had sent off a new supply of pine needles for Vita's Queen Victoria–Prince Albert pillow. Her letter also mentioned the birth of her son Benedict's daughter, as well as her concern over the Suez crisis, a concern heightened by the fact that her son Nigel, the Member of Parliament for Bournemouth East, was taking the unpopular stand of opposing the government's policy.

August 11, 1956

Dearest Andrew

. . . .

The same day as the pillow my second grand-daughter arrived into this world—a little half Italian baby, to be called Vanessa Pepita.

We have been having the most appalling storms; gales of wind, real hurricanes, and torrents of rain. Tunbridge Wells, which is only 15 miles from here, was buried three foot deep in hail-stones. It looked as though it were under snow. Luckily we escaped the hail, but my poor garden looks very battered, and the damage to the Kent orchards is incalculable. Also to the hops gardens.

. . . .

I am busy ordering bulbs to grow in bowls for the house. Of course we are all very worried over the Suez Canal business, but one must carry on with life just the same and pray that we do not get precipitated into another war to destroy us all this time. Now I must stop because it is Saturday, and the post goes early, but I did want to write at once and thank you for a very precious present.

With love
Vita

A feature of Andrew's life at Windslip not previously mentioned in the correspondence was his pack of standard poodles. Her novel *The Easter Party* had testified to Vita's lifelong fondness for dogs, so Andrew did not hesitate to tell her of his sorrow at the death of one of his. Vita replied sympathetically, "I have been through the same misery many times in a long dog-ridden life, and I know what it is like." This letter of September 22 also contained domestic news.

Vanessa was christened two days ago, Vanessa Pepita Giovanna. She has a godfather aged 91, old Bernhard [Bernard] Berenson the art critic, for whom Luisa worked and who is a great friend of hers and Ben's.

No, they didn't call her after Vanessa Bell (nee Stephen.) It was just that they liked the name and wanted something that would go both in English and Italian.

FRIENDSHIP

The last page of the letter was a melodrama:

You nearly lost your friend Vita last week. I got stung by a wasp, and had to be rushed by ambulance to the nearest hospital as they thought they might have to cut my throat open. I couldn't breathe. However, all was well, but it is a nuisance being so allergic to wasps. I very nearly died some years ago of the same thing.

My poor dog Rollo panicked when he saw me being carried off on a stretcher, and took to the woods and they had all the trouble in the world getting him to come home.

I am quite all right again so don't waste any sympathy on me.

Vita's Christmas letter began with one of her rare references to politics. She, like Harold, was appalled by Britain's part in the Suez crisis. Happily, there was also the more encouraging news of Harold's seventieth birthday present to occupy her mind. A group of his friends had raised a subscription to give him a check for £1370, which was to be used for a cruise.[20] The story of that trip is told in his book *Journey to Java*.

December 4, 1956

Dearest Andrew

I think it is about time I wrote you a letter for Christmas. I hope you are not as cross with me as your President is cross with my country men? I won't write to you about politics, and won't make any comments on the things that are happening in the world—that would be a foolish waste of paper. All I can say, is that it is a tragic pity that there should be any division or misunderstanding between America and ourselves. We depend on one another, and I pray that the temporary breach may be repaired.

Meanwhile, I send you my good wishes and affection for Christmas. I wonder how you spend your Christmas? You may be under snow. We may also be under snow, but I hope not.

I must tell you that we may possibly be going away on a cruise in January and February. We wanted to, but couldn't afford it. So a lot of Harold's friends got up a subscription to give him a cheque on his 70th birthday, and have subscribed enough to pay for a cruise. It is most touching of them. I don't know where we will go, all the ships seem to be booked up. We might go down the coast of South America. I would like the Caribbean myself, but one can't get booking at this late date.

Anyhow, I daresay we will obtain something or other, and meanwhile it is rather exciting to feel one may be going off at a moment's notice.

But this letter is really meant to bring you my Christmas wishes, dear Andrew, from your unknown distant friend.

Vita

Andrew sent Vita a parcel of American cigarettes, which arrived at Sissinghurst on Christmas Eve. She wrote immediately to thank him.

I wish I could visualize you in your home at Christmas. Harold and I will be alone (which we like) and I suppose someone will stick up a few sprigs of holly in the dining room; otherwise it will be just like any other day—except for some coloured paper strewn about, off parcels—and string—and envelopes—and a mess all over the floor—and Harold will say "Thank goodness that's over," and will go away leaving me to clear up.

I send you my best wishes for next year, dear Andrew, and may it bring peace and better understanding between nations. We all make mistakes, don't we?

Even the good wishes of the festive season could not lessen the soreness of the Suez situation.

The journey to Java was to be the first of six winter cruises for the Nicolsons. These trips served the dual purpose of providing relief from the severe cold at Sissinghurst and giving Vita and Harold perfect conditions for working holidays. They could enjoy long hours for reading and writing, a luxury not to be found in the midst of busy Sissinghurst and London lives. Travel had always been an important part of Vita's experience, although in late years her trips had been confined to Europe. This first leisurely cruise to the Far East was a source of great delight for her. She did not, however, forget to write to her friend Andrew.

SS William Ruys, in the
Indian Ocean
February 29th, 1957

Dearest Andrew

I ought to have written to you before now, but it did seem so impossibly far away, and also I have been disheartened by all the mails going astray, I now hear from home that you have sent me a lovely Valentine of zinnia seeds; you *are* kind again; I look forward to finding them when I get back on March 17th. (I shall post this at Cape Town.)

We have had a wonderful journey, all round by Indonesia, Malaya, and Ceylon. This last island is beautiful, so green and luxuriant, and it is fun to meet an elephant strolling casually along the road. In Java we stayed with some English people up in the mountains, on a tea and rubber estate; that was fun too, and it took us right away into the country, far from the noise and heat and dust of Djakarta. (Djakarta is the capital of Java, a beastly place). It has been, and still is, very hot; rather too hot for my liking at times; but both Harold and I have managed to do a lot of work, writing in our cabins all morning and again most of the evening. Our fellow passengers who never do anything but gossip, play bridge, or turn over the pages of old magazines, probably think us quite mad.

And how have you been faring, I wonder? Frozen out, and lots of snow? In England they appear to have had the mildest spring on record, with everything three weeks in advance of what it ought to be; I tremble to think what will happen to all the tender shoots if winter weather descends on England now. They say there are floods everywhere, and over Europe too. We shall have no petrol, or very little; never mind, it will be lovely to be home.

> With much love from
> Vita

One of her first tasks on her return home was a scribbled note to Andrew.

> March 19, 1957

Andrew, I got home last night. I found your zinnias and your letter. (I found almost two months worth of correspondence waiting for me, but most of that I can answer through my secretary) but your letter I must answer personally.

Posts went terribly wrong on our voyage, and we now know that we lost a lot of letters. Thus, I never got your Valentine sent to Java. We never got a whole lot of others sent to the addresses we had given.

Anyhow, we are back—and it was a lovely voyage—and we both enjoyed it and profited from it, and feel all the better from it. I didn't write any poetry (since you ask) but I did write a lot of a prose book, a biography. It was so peaceful on the ship, we had time to write. No interruptions, no responsibilities—just hours and hours of peace.

> Love
> Vita

The biography to which she referred was *Daughter of France*, a biography of Anne Marie Louise d'Orleans, Duchesse de Montpensier, known to history as "La Grande Mademoiselle." The book proved to be a very difficult one for Vita to write. She had begun it in 1947 but did not publish it until 1959.

Vita's next letter began with a familiar complaint against the speed of the passage of time. Summer was, of course, the busy season for the garden, and this year she had staff difficulties to cope with, as well as the usual influx of visitors.

June 30, 1957

Dearest Andrew

I do not suppose you will ever wish to speak to me again, I have been so bad about writing. I simply do not know how the days go by, but here we are at the end of June and I must have owed you a letter for at least 2 months. The fact is that apart from my ordinary (and manifold) occupations, I lost my head gardener in the middle of April and am left with two men, which isn't nearly enough for this garden, so I do as much as I can myself, and moreover I have to supervise them,—act as head gardener myself, in short,—so I spend every free minute trying to prevent my garden from getting into too much of a mess. It is very difficult nowadays to get a really good head-gardener, the breed seems to be extinct, but I have found one at last and I hope he will arrive within a week.

. . . .

The zinnias are coming up grandly in spite of an unusually prolonged drought. Not in flower yet but that's all to the good. We are having a heat wave, and both H. and

I have gone back into our tropical clothes. The temperature goes up to over 90, which is high for England. I water frantically in the early morning and late evening, to keep some things alive.

The industrious Harold has just finished another book, called *Journey to Java*, which may amuse you to read. He said to me somewhat alarmingly "I hope you won't mind being used as comic relief." I assured him that I should not mind at all.

What a terrible disaster you have had in Louisiana. I do hope the coast of Maine isn't subject to hurricanes and tidal waves, but I think Windslip stands safely high above the sea?

We have had such a lot of Americans here this summer (to our garden, I mean;) recently the du Ponts, who have that amazing garden near Wilmington,—at least, two of the young du Ponts; of course Harry du Pont is dead, leaving the garden to the nation. Very nice they were, and my word how rich they must be! They were 'doing' Europe with two daughters, and came in the largest car I have ever seen.

Well I suppose I must go and pull up a few more weeds, on this hot Sunday morning, dear Andrew. . . .

> With love,
> V.

The delightful travel journal *Journey to Java* that Harold produced so rapidly upon his return from the cruise did, in fact, contain many references to Vita's idiosyncrasies. His notion of "comic relief," however, proved in this instance to be instead affection and mild amusement. Two passages from the section

headed "Tuesday, February 26th," just the day before Vita
wrote to Andrew, are typical of Harold's treatment of her and
their relationship. The first concerns the usual morning routine
of writing in the cabin; the second, speculations occasioned by
an afterdinner stroll on the deck.

It is very hot but not as calm as yesterday. V. is convinced
that the air pumped into her cabin through the orifices of the
air-conditioning machine is "unnatural," and that if she opens
the window onto the flaming sea she will acquire God's air,
which is purer and cooler. She does so, with the result that the
thermometer in her cabin rapidly jumps up two degrees. She
then closes her cabin window, adjusts the nozzles of the air-
conditioning machine, and settles down to *La Grande
Mademoiselle*, with her books of reference and her notes spread
like a picnic on the bunk beside her.[21]

As we walk back along the deck we pause as always to gaze at
the stars. V. remarks that one of the mistakes of Nature is to
have provided the earth with but a single satellite when she
might just as well have given us the nine that she accorded to
Jupiter. How wonderful it would be, when ploughing on a calm
night through the Indian Ocean, if we could see nine moons
above us, radiant in the luminous sky. They would whirl around
us like globes, like crescents, or like gibbous lights. I remark that
if this were so, it would be even more difficult than it is today to
calculate the tides at London Bridge. Moreover, even as the
Pacific Ocean was formed by the moon leaving us, so also might
two whole continents swing away from us to form these satel-
lites. "It might be America!" she remarks hopefully. "Or
Eurasia," I add with equal hope. What I like about V. is that
she is always having odd ideas. What have I done, O mighty
Poseidon! to deserve so entrancing a companion?[22]

FRIENDSHIP

Back at Sissinghurst, by late August the Andrew zinnias were in full bloom and Vita reported on them to Andrew:

> There's my garden crammed with peppermint-stick zin-nias, all thanks to you. I get up early in the morning to pick them for my own room. It is a room that takes flowers in a very lovely way, if you know what I mean. Some rooms take flowers better than others. My room is an odd room. Its walls are of rough Tudor brick—date about 1540. When I first came to live here they were covered in hideous wall-paper: I stripped it off, intending to distemper it, but then found the old brick so pretty that I left it all rough as it was, the color of pot-pourri,—a sort of half-pink, half-grey, and mottled.
>
> Incidentally, stripping off the wallpaper revealed a huge fireplace and a pointed window, hitherto concealed.

Accompanying her description of the room are two rough sketches with the notation "only I can't draw, so forgive." On November 11, Vita wrote to Andrew to give him her itinerary for that winter's cruise, this time to Peru and Chile. The trip was spoiled by illness for her, occasioned perhaps by the tooth extraction she wrote him of. She had learned of Russia's successful launching of Sputnik on October 5, and both she and Harold were greatly excited by it.

> I have been feeling pretty miserable because I had an impacted wisdom tooth which meant an hour and a half on the operating table and left me with a lot of my jaw sawn away—and very sore altogether! I was two nights in a nursing home—very cross at the waste of time when I have

Sissinghurst

Aug. 24. 1957.

Dearest Andrew – how endlessly
kind you are to me – A huge
box arrived, full of Pepitas;
I can't think why you should be
so kind and generous – and
there's my garden crammed
with peppermint-stick-zinnias,
all thanks to you – I get up
early in the morning to pick
them for my own room. It is
a room that takes flowers in a
very lovely way – if you know
what I mean. Some rooms
take flowers better than others –
My room is an odd room. Its

Pages one and two of Vita's letter of August 24, 1957.

walls are of rough Tudor brick –
date about 1540 –   When I first
came to live here they were covered in
hideous wall-paper ; I stripped it off,
just intending to distemper it, but then
found the old brick so pretty that I
left it all rough as it was,
the colour of pot-pourri, – sort of
half-brick, half-gray, and
mottled –
      Incidentally, stripping off the
wall paper revealed a huge fireplace
and a pointed window, hitherto
concealed –

picture of
fire place.

picture
of window

Only I can't
draw – so
forgive.

much to do before going away—and am losing my secretary who is getting married. Still, if she is going to be happy. . . . But it's a bore for me, having to start afresh with a stranger. She naturally knew all about everything, after years here, and was invaluable, besides being *so* nice and getting on well with everybody. I think the young man (a doctor) is very lucky, and I would willingly wring his neck. They will go to live in South Africa so we shall lose her altogether.

What other news have I for you? My boy Nigel had a son this autumn, called Adam, so I have now three grandchildren. But that's merely personal. The big bit of news of course has been the Sputnik, with the whole British nation getting hysterical over the dog. Poor little creature, I feel as sorry for it as anybody, but the indignation has really been a bit out of proportion. However, it does credit to our kind humane hearts.

Well dear Andrew here's a happy Christmas for you. I shall be spending mine in Cartagena, Colombia!

Love
Vita

Vita wrote on December 24 to tell Andrew of her illness and to thank him for his Christmas present, a "grand lip-stick."

Dearest Andrew

How funny to be writing to you from Venezuela, which always sounded to me like a place that didn't really exist.

I have two letters from you to answer: one which I got the very day I left Sissinghurst and one which much to my surprise I found at Havana. I ought to have answered them both before now, but first we ran into a truly appalling storm with a 100 m.p.h. gale, and secondly I've been ill with a mysterious fever until two or three days ago when I began to shake it off,—I hope for ever. It really laid me out. . . .

It has been very hot and calm and lovely these last few days. I have not been well enough to go ashore anywhere yet, but I don't really mind, as we call at the same places on the way back, and it is really rather pleasant and peaceful having the ship practically to oneself for a few hours, and then hearing other people's accounts of what they have seen on land.

I hope this may reach you by New Years Day to bring you the best of good wishes. I shall post it in Curaçao because they say the Venezuelan post is totally unreliable. You know that it does really bring you very very warm wishes not only for New Years Day but for the whole of 1958, dear Andrew,

from
Vita

Andrew attempted to cheer up Vita's convalescence by sending her a humorous telegram to the ship signed "Andrew Culpeper." Culpeper was the last name of the strange little man whom Harold introduced into his *Journey to Java* as a foil. Vita sent her appreciation of the joke and further wishes for the New Year on a postcard from Cartagena.

The Nicolsons returned to England on February 9. Vita wrote Andrew on the twenty-second, ". . . You can imagine the confusion I've been in after 2½ months (nearly) away, stacks

Vita's postcard to Andrew from Cartagena, Colombia.

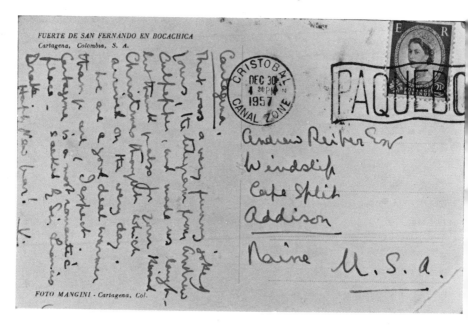

of correspondence, everyone waiting to fall on me like a pack of wolves, and my secretary in process of getting married." She mentioned the second part of the cruise, which was much more eventful than the first for everyone. "We struck another terrific storm on the way home, after Bermuda—also a revolution in Venezuela, so couldn't go up to Caracas where they were machine-gunning in the streets. I wanted to go, but no one was allowed on shore." It is easy to imagine romantic Vita being caught up by the excitement of a revolution and ignoring the obvious danger of the situation.

The weather and its effect on her garden, even more than on people, were also on her mind on her return to Sissinghurst.

From what I read in the papers, I fear you must have been having a terrible spell of winter. I hope your house is solid and that you are able to keep warm? Knowing American efficiency in that direction, I expect you are. It is more than I can say for the English, whose pipes burst with the utmost regularity every year and who never do anything preventive about it.

Some daffodils are already out, and masses of crocuses, little irises etc. I think we must get the beginnings of spring earlier than you do. It is nice to have the house full of flowers without stint.

Vita's next letter is dated "March 21st (meant to be the first day of Spring, but white with snow.)" The cold was the main theme of her letter. What progress spring had made in February seems to have been counteracted by unusually wintry weather the next month.

I see you are again having winter weather, and I suppose you'll pass it on to us, across the Atlantic, as you usually do. We have been simply frozen, here,—my hand so cold I could hardly hold a pen. This, I suppose, is unknown to you with central heating, and must seem utterly barbarous. I couldn't agree more.

Impossible to do anything in the garden. The ground is hard and cold. The few daffodils that have come out lie flat on the grass, sparkling in the frost and looking like crystallized apricots. However, it is bound to change soon.

In April, Vita received a newspaper clipping from Andrew about a neighbor of his on Cape Split, Susie Thompson, a Maine native who had taken up watercolor painting late in life but who displayed an extraordinary talent for catching the essence of the beauty surrounding her. Vita was perhaps more intrigued by the information that the newspaper provided about Andrew than about Susie.

The cutting about Susie Thompson amused me very much. She must be a sort of second Grandma Moses. How clever of you, my art patron, to spot her talent and encourage her. But what amused me most about it was to discover that you have been "a one-time motion picture actor and theatre official." Also that you were "a native of New Orleans." I never knew anything of this. Do you really come from the Deep South? It was one of my greatest regrets that I never got there, when I toured a vast area of U.S.A. lecturing in 1933. I got right across the Middle West (including Denver) and to California, but never down south where I passionately wanted to go. South Carolina was my furthest south and very nice too. I loved Charleston.

She continued the letter to give Andrew her usual homely news from her garden.

It is nearly Easter, which I always think the loveliest feast in the Calendar, but we are still shivering in an icy East wind and getting some degrees of frost every night. Did I tell you that I have got two squirrels who come into my bedroom every morning at daybreak, and play about all over my window sill and table, and scamper over my room? I put nuts for them,—very silly of me, as they are terribly destructive in a garden and ought to be shot,—and as there are two of them there will soon be at least four babies,—but I do rather love watching them as I lie in bed reading. They have become so tame—and chatter furiously at me when the supply of nuts runs out. My dog, strangely enough, takes no notice of them whatsoever; I think he pretends not to know they are there. More dignified.

Vita's next letter, dated July 20, was a variation on a familiar theme—where did time go? She concluded her musing: "One should not attempt to be an ordinary person and a writer at the same time! The two things are incompatible and irreconcilable." And once again she was moved to mention the worrisome political situation that intruded even on the peace of her Kentish countryside.

We have had a bad summer of wind and rain, and now we have all this disquieting news from the Near East, but at least this time we are collaborating openly with yourselves and doing it in a legal sort of way, not like that disgraceful episode of Suez. I only hope to God it quietens down before we all blow each other to bits. I don't in the least want to die just yet, do you? No I am sure you don't: you find too much to enjoy in life, and so do I.

Many times in their correspondence Vita compared her life to Andrew's. At a distance it seemed to her that he must lead an especially tranquil life, uninterrupted by the various kinds of demands she suffered from. So it always seems to one who looks in from outside on another's life. On September 4, in a letter to thank him for a new box of Pepita nuts, she wrote: "I wonder how you spend your days. It must be a very peaceful existence, and I suppose that now in September everything will be beginning to turn those wonderful colours I have heard so much of. Then you will have your hard winter, when you have to shut yourself warmly indoors—and I [expect] you read a lot, but what else do you do?"

At this time Vita was feeling particularly pressed by her biography of the Grande Mademoiselle. She had in fact written the last words of it on August 13, but much remained to be done. "I have nearly finished my book; in fact I *have* finished it, but with a biography there is always a lot of tidying up to do,—appendixes, indexes, biographical notes, etc. all very boring, but necessary. It's not like a novel, which is really finished once one has written the last words. My book won't come out till January or February, while I'm away. We don't get back till March."

The absence she referred to was occasioned by the third winter cruise that the Nicolsons were planning.

Did I tell you that H. and I were going a long sea-journey again this winter? We leave directly after Christmas, (personally I wish it were *before* Christmas) and go to China and Japan on a French Boat, the Cambodge of the Messageries Maritimes. On the way, we go to Manila and Saigon. Perhaps I told you all this before; if so, forgive me. I think it should be fun, except that I hate leaving my dog! He stays with a very nice friend of mine, who lives only a mile from here, and is quite happy, so I ought not to mind.

She ended her letter with: "Well, I must go and have my supper now as it is after 10 P.M. and I've been working ever since 5 and am hungry. . . ."

Vita had also inquired after Susie Thompson in that letter. So, with his usual ingenuity, Andrew contrived to have a friend take one of Susie Thompson's watercolors to Vita during the autumn. She was delighted with the gift. "What a lovely wild coast, and how magnificently she has caught the spirit of it! I shall certainly get it framed in the way you suggest, very simple, with some pale colour to pick up the colour of sea and sky."

Andrew was most interested in Vita's proposed visit to Angkor during her approaching cruise, and mentioned to her a book that she might find profitable to consult. She replied:

Harold gave me a superb book recently published, with dozens of full-page photographs. He gave it me for the 45th anniversary of our wedding! October 1st. So you see how old we are, but you can also see that he never forgets, which I find very touching after so long. Do you know, Andrew, that in all those years, we have never once had a row? or even what is called "words"? I doubt if many people could say as much, or they might say it, but not with truth.

She ended this letter of October 21st with an amusing speculation:

What a jig-saw puzzle to correlate your life and mine! So different. We probably both make quite a wrong picture. It's rather like a Henry James story.

Knowing that the Nicolsons planned to leave on their cruise immediately after Christmas day, Andrew sent his Christmas present early that year, another "lovely luxurious lip-stick," a gift occasioned originally by Ann Merriam's somewhat critical observation of Vita's preferences in cosmetics. Vita's thank-you note included the itinerary of their trip and her appreciation for the gift. "So smart! You don't know what an untidy old gipsy I am, and this lip-stick will grand me up, as Harold says of the flag I fly on the tower: 'It grands the place up.'"

The cruise to the Far East was far more successful than the previous year's had been. Vita wrote to Andrew on February 3, as the ship lay off the coast of Formosa.

The high-lights of the journey have been Ceylon and Hong Kong. Ceylon I had loved the first time I went there, and loved all over again the second time. It really is a dream of an island.

Hong Kong was quite unexpectedly beautiful. The town itself is quite good fun in the Chinese streets, but when you get away from the town into the country it is even better, with hilly roads and marvellous views over sea and islands. We had friends there, with motor cars, so we really did see everything there was to be seen in the two and a half days. On the return journey we hope to go out to Macao, which is an old Portuguese settlement about 3 hours by boat from Hong Kong. A most eccentric Englishman has very kindly lent us his house there, complete with motor-car and servants, so we shall spend the night there in peace. Our host, who appears to have houses in odd places all over the world, will be absent, which is just as well as he gets embarrassingly drunk.

It is indeed queer to think of you sitting in the middle of snow and ice flows (?floes), when we have been so hot we didn't know what to do with ourselves. I lost my little Spanish fan somewhere, but have now got an enormous Chinese one. It is cooler now that we have got out of the tropics. In Japan we go to Kobe, Kyoto, Yokohama, and Tokyo, and quite enough too: that country does not attract me in the least, nor do its inhabitants.

Despite the Nicolsons' delight in their holiday, they were worried again about the career of Nigel, their younger son. Once more he had taken a stance immensely unpopular with his constituents, and was in danger of losing his seat in Parliament. "My poor Nigel seems to be having a lovely time over his politics. I wonder if you happened to see a recent copy of 'Time' which had a longish article about it all? The English press has been full of it, but I didn't expect it to have echoes in America."

The Nicolsons reached Sissinghurst again in early March. Vita wrote Andrew on March 14.

My homecoming hasn't been too happy, because while I was still away I heard that my beautiful and beloved Alsatian had suddenly developed a tumor on the liver and there was nothing to be done except put him to sleep—but I miss him quite dreadfully. He wasn't young, nearly eleven, and something was bound to have happened before long, but it's a very horrid blank all the same.

She was also extremely worried by the controversy raging over the publication by Nigel's firm of Weidenfeld and Nicolson of the novel *Lolita* by the excellent Russian novelist Vladimir Nabokov.

I wonder if you have got hold of a copy of Lolita yet? You said you were trying to. I think it is a revolting book, and am very angry at Nigel having got involved in it. His partners arranged to publish it, and he had never even read it—so of course knew nothing about it till this storm burst over them. I haven't seen Nigel as he is in Germany, but he has written copiously to tell us about everything while we have been away, so we are well up to date with his battles of one sort and another.

Despite all the news, Vita, as usual, was rushed. She ended: "Dear Andrew, I've got 2½ months of correspondence etc to deal with—perhaps you can imagine the pile—so no more for the moment, but I had to write to you priority to thank you for everything and above all for your affection,—quite undeserved." Vita was ill for two months that spring. On April 22 she wrote Andrew a sad little letter.

Dearest Andrew

I have been rather ill (and am still in bed) with a horrid thing called Virus pneumonia—which gives you a raging temperature and makes you feel awful. I am better now, but still get some fever every night so they won't let me get up till I shake it off completely. You can imagine how I rage at missing all the spring and not being able to see my garden which everyone tells me is looking lovely. It is *maddening!*

. . . .

Have not much news, having been laid up for nearly three weeks. I couldn't even read much at first, but the wireless is a great resource. I think people who are normally very strong and healthy make extremely bad patients: they can't resign themselves to having the whole of their life upset, and of course from a practical point of view it *is* very inconvenient,—I mean, I have masses of things I ought to see to personally and there is no one to take my place—and the doctor says it will be the middle of May before I am really fit again.

Dear me, what a grumble. You must forgive me.

I hope that you at least are enjoying the spring, which must be beautiful on your wild coast.

Ever affectionately
Vita

She was still bedridden in May and on the eighth wrote Andrew another letter from her bedroom.

Dearest Andrew

I got your letter this morning. . . . I was thrilled to read of your yellow erythroniums,[23] fancy their growing wild! Do you also have trilliums? The Trinity flower. If only there wasn't so much bother about importing bulbs, I should beg you to dig up some of the erythroniums, but they would only stick in the Customs.

I am still ill, which is maddening—over five weeks now, and missing all the spring and the garden. I was getting better, and then a lot of people came and I got over-tired, and the beastly thing seized upon me again. However, I

seem to be getting better again now. It was my own fault really, as the doctor warned me, but it is so difficult to be firm with people—and one is at their mercy. I also had to chuck the gala performance at Covent Garden for the Shah of Persia, to which we had been invited. But I minded that less than not being able to get out into the garden.

So you may imagine that I have not any news to speak of. I just lie here, and try to see what I can of the garden out of the window. Friends come to see me, but I am not really allowed visitors, and I can't say I want them much for after talking ten minutes or so I begin to feel exhausted.

Silly, isn't it? and oh what a waste of time.

I hope that you at least are well and enjoying the beginning of summer.

. . . .

Now I do apologize for writing a second dull invalidish letter, but my head is made of cotton wool.

Yours,
V.

By July, Vita had almost recovered, although she still had to be very careful not to overtire herself. Andrew had, of course, picked up on her mention of the yellow erythronium and promised to smuggle a root into England for her.

July 6, 1959

Dearest Andrew

I hope your erythronium friend will find his way here when he comes over for the lily conference. It would be very thrilling to have some bulbs from America. The English catalogues don't list Erythronium *americanum*, but I daresay it is the same thing under a different name.

I wonder if you have seen anything of the excitement over the Queen's visit to Canada. It sounds to me the most strenuous tour anyone has ever undertaken. What people don't realise is that in her so-called off-time for rest and relaxation, she has a mass of business to attend to, and thus really never gets any rest at all. And it has been so hot! It has been very hot here too,—90° in the shade.

You will be amused to hear that H. and I were invited to go on an American luxury yacht in September for a cruise calling at the Maine ports. It belongs to a Mrs. Aldritch. I must say I was rather tempted, but I don't think I could stand the pace of American life and whoopee. But wouldn't you have been surprised if we had turned up at Cape Split?

The Pepitas are delicious, everyone is amused by them—I occasionally have two or three people for drinks in the evening, and produce the Pepitas then. I get them warmed up in the oven. One man thought I was offering them to him to grow in his garden.

I am gradually getting better, but still have to go very slow or I get completely exhausted; these viruses are the very devil. There is a theory that they may have come over from the concentration camps in Europe. I don't think anybody really knows very much about it. I heard of a boy who got the same thing as I, and took *six months* to get over it—so I've been lucky with only 3½ months so far.

I wonder how you occupy yourself these summer days? Do you garden? and read a lot, I expect.

Love from
V.

It took nearly six months for the erythronium to arrive at Sissinghurst, but arrive they did, legally or not, in the company of some trillium. Vita wrote on December 16:

The most wonderful rich package of trillium and erythronium·has miraculously arrived, and they have been planted with the utmost care, with some spent hops mixed in with the soil. "Spent hops" may puzzle you: it means the hops we get from the brewers after they have been used for beer. We who live in hop-country are fortunate in being able to get this valuable form of manure; we can get it for nothing except the cost of transport, which as you may imagine is very little.

Anyway, your present couldn't have been given a better start in life—nor could it have been more appreciated.

Andrew was always alert for any reference to Vita, her garden, and her writing in the American press. On July 5 the *Boston Sunday Globe* carried a page of pictures of Sissinghurst. The accompanying text, written by Gordon Langley Hall, was entitled "Britain's Rose Queen."

That is what they call her, and surely nobody is more deserving of the name, for Vita Sackville-West, poet and novelist, literally turned a wilderness into one of the world's great gardens. Set in the green heart of Kent about 30 miles from Canterbury, Sissinghurst Castle and its flowers draw visitors from all parts of the world every year. Yet only thirty years ago Sissinghurst lay hidden beneath a tangled mass of briar and bramble. Then the property was rescued by Miss Sackville-West, and with the aid of her husband, Sir Harold Nicolson, diplomat and author, the beautiful gardens once more came into their own. Sir Harold planned them—his wife planted them.

Sissinghurst Castle was built shortly before 1550, and went into decline after it was used to house French soldiers seized in North America during the Seven Years' War. Later, it became a poorhouse and then a group of farm workers' cottages. Today the orchard is filled with hundreds of varieties of rose bushes.

Countless other plants blaze in season, pigeons nest among the chimneys, and in her tower Britain's Rose Queen works quietly at her writing.

On July 26, Vita replied to Andrew's query about the article.

Yes, I did see the article about Britain's Rose Queen. The joke is that Gordon Langley Hall (known to his friends as Dinkie) is the son of my chauffeur. He is the most extraordinary young man, and has managed to get himself adopted as her son and heir by a Miss Isabel Whitney, who provides him with an 8-room flat in New York, a secretary (male), and a housekeeper (female). He is very good to his real mother, and has bought her a house not far from here for her old age. It has a garden, and he gets a bunch of flowers flown once a week to New York, to lay at the feet of a statue of St. Teresa of Avila. He has written several books, gives lectures, speaks on the American wireless, and is quite a successful journalist. At one moment he was a schoolmaster at a lumber camp in the north of Canada. A most fantastic creature. He comes home here from time to time.

We have had a marvellous summer, hot and dry. The gardens are completely burnt up. I am very much better, in fact almost well, so can enjoy it. Lots of people come, which is a very easy and agreeable way of seeing one's friends—no effort and no obligation. It's like having a continuous garden party. . . . Amongst other people we had the du Ponts, who have what must be a wonderful garden in Delaware,—nice, simple, unpretentious people whom you would never suspect of being millionaires.

If my *Nursery Rhymes* is still in print I will send you a copy. *Heritage* and *Challenge* are long since out of print, and very bad anyway. *Heritage* was the first novel I ever wrote.

The autumn of 1959 was enlivened by the production of a play, *The Edwardians*, adapted from Vita's best-selling novel of 1930. It opened at the Theatre Royal, Windsor, and then moved to London's Saville Theatre on October 15. The lead role of Sebastian was played by Jeremy Brett, the role of Vigeon the butler by the veteran actor Ernest Thesiger, and that of the dowager by Athene Seyler. The settings were by Michael Eve and Hal Henshaw. Vita was amused by the entire venture and also rather surprised by the success of the play. Two of her letters concern the production.

On October 3, she wrote:

I have no news, except that my book *The Edwardians* has been dramatised and has been a great success at a provincial theatre (at Windsor) where it was tried out last month, and is coming to London on October 15th. I can't think why it has been a success, because I thought it pretty poor myself, and fully expect it to be a flop in London. There is some very good acting in it—Ernest Thesiger and Athene Seyler, if those names convey anything to you. I know you have an interest in the theatre still.

Well, we shall see. I expect it will come off after a week's run.

Then on November 5, she remarked:

The play is still running, rather to my surprise as I thought it awfully bad. The set is pretty enough, though not by Cecil Beaton. It is the garden front of Knole. The women's clothes are very pretty, by Gladys Calthorp, who happens to be a friend of mine and has done a lot of work for Noel Coward.

But it seems impossible to get modern actors to play at being aristocrats of 1910: they just haven't the manner. The young man who plays the duke might be a shop-assistant. The only one who is really right is Ernest Thesiger as the old family butler. But then not only is he 80 years old, but he is a gentleman by birth and knows what's what.

My first and only plunge into the theatrical world has amused me vastly. I feel I have had to learn a new language. Not that I've had very much to do with the play, perhaps a pity I didn't do more!

Vita's December letter gave Andrew the itinerary for their projected tour to South Africa. "Harold and I are off directly after Christmas, down the east coast of Africa. We are not looking forward to it very much, but at least it will be warm." The cruise turned out to be much more enjoyable than Vita had anticipated. She wrote Andrew on February 2 from Mombasa:

Well, we are now homeward bound, and although I have enjoyed this cruise so far I am never sorry to get home. There is a terrible sameness about the African ports, with the exception of Cape Town. The only really amusing and picturesque place we went to was Zanzibar, an old Arab town on a very beautiful and fertile island. Did you ever go there? I should love to know where your travels had taken you.

They don't usually call at Zanzibar unless they have a lot

of cargo or passengers, but we coaxed the captain who is an old darling into going off his course, and had a whole day there. Did you know that nearly all the cloves in the world grow on trees in Zanzibar? It was fun to see them all drying on mats by the roadside in the sun.

My word, it was hot! It's pretty hot here too; we are nearing the Equator. But the ship is beautifully air-conditioned, so one can always come down to one's cabin to get cool. H. and I spend a lot of time in our separate cabins; he is writing a book on the 18th century and I have more frivolously been writing a novel.

We get home on the 19th, but if you felt so inclined you could write to me c/o Miss Freya Stark, . . . Italy, where we shall be staying on the 16th and 17th. It would be nice to find a word from you waiting there.

From that last paragraph it seems clear that Vita had not forgotten Andrew's habit of sending her a note on their special holiday, St. Valentine's Day. The novel that Vita was writing on board ship was *No Signposts in the Sea*, which is set against a cruise. Published in 1961, it was her last novel.

As usual, Vita was delighted to return home to Sissinghurst. She wrote Andrew on February 21:

It's cold here, after the Equator. But I think it was even colder in Venice where we had thick fog, and in Asolo where Freya lives, where it snowed heavily all day. I am always glad to be home, and my little dog Dan was so pleased to see me. I quite thought he would have forgotten me, as he was young and I had sent him away to be looked after during my absence, but he hadn't forgotten at all and simply hurled himself into my arms. I believe you like

cats: I prefer dogs. Dan is a black and white Border collie; I
didn't get another Alsatian after my beloved Rollo died last
year.

There are snowdrops and aconites and crocuses out in
the garden and some flowering shrubs, so it's not looking
too grim. Your erythronium have been so carefully
planted in a prepared bed; they are not showing through
yet, but I hope they are happy underneath. I will write and
tell you about them when they flower. Did I tell you I now
had two young women as gardeners? Highly trained, and
perfectly excellent. The garden is a dream of tidiness; all I
hope is that they haven't tidied everything away forever in
an excess of zeal.

Vita was always busy with many journalistic chores, in addi-
tion to her famous garden series in the *Observer*. She wrote to
Andrew next on March 4 of a congenial assignment: "I am
going down to Gloucestershire for a couple of nights, because I
have been asked to write a new guidebook to one of the most
romantic and historical houses in England: Berkeley Castle. I
don't know if you know about it. It is where Edward II was
murdered, and it is referred to in Shakespeare, and was besieged
by Cromwell, so you see lots of English history and literature is
bound up with it."

FRIENDSHIP

In April Andrew received a letter from a Vita in first a playful, then a musing mood. It began: "Dear Prince Andrew, Sir:
my humble duty to your royal highness, and the usual apologies
for being so remiss a correspondent." At the end of the letter she
wrote, "I try so often to visualise your life: it must be so different
from mine, and I don't suppose you can visualise mine any
better than I can visualise yours. Never mind: we are very good
friends aren't we? even without ever having seen each other."

Farewell

1961–1962

WALTER SINCLAIR, Andrew's companion, had fallen ill the previous year. Andrew had first written to Vita of his illness in the autumn of 1959, and had kept her apprised of his progress since then. But in June of 1960, Andrew informed her of Walter Sinclair's death. Vita wrote in sympathy:

> How can I tell you how sorry I feel for you? After so many years of close companionship you must indeed feel desolate. I had so hoped he was getting better.
>
> . . . .
>
> I wonder what you will do now? I hope it doesn't mean that you must leave your home and all your familiar surroundings? But will you feel too lonely there, with no one to share it with?

And you will have all the painful aftermath to cope with,—the personal possessions, all the endless small things that remind you at every turn of your loss.

Dear Andrew, I feel for you and can enter into your feelings almost as vividly as though I were there.

With love and infinite sympathy,

Vita.

She repeated her inquiries about Andrew's future in July, when she wrote him from her bed, where she was confined by a recurrence of viral pneumonia.

I do so wonder what your future is going to be? Shall you stay on alone at Windslip? or shall you import another friend to share it with? It would be lonely for you, surely, all by yourself? but I can't imagine you anywhere else. All your roots must be there.

I am afraid you must be feeling very desolate and unhappy. I know you have many good friends, but some people are irreplaceable—after many close years together—so what will you do?

Love from
Vita

Since Harold's two slight strokes in 1955, both Nicolsons had been uncomfortably aware of their decline in health and the approach of death. Vita had written to Harold on November 8 of the year that Walter Sinclair died: "And now, in our advancing age, we love each other more deeply than ever, and also more agonisingly, since we see the inevitable end. It is not nice to know that one of us must die before the other." [24]

Probably because of her own concern over Harold's health, she was especially interested in Andrew's grief and the way in which he coped with it. She certainly empathized with him in the loss of his life's companion. On November 19 she wrote:

I am glad you have two poodles. Dogs are such extraordinarily comforting company, making no demands and giving silent sympathy. I am sure they know when one is sad.

Are you alone at Windslip? I know you have lots of friends, but I meant alone in the house.

Again, in her Christmas letter of December 21, she wrote:

I am afraid you will have a lonely Christmas, in spite of the two poodles. Dogs are nice; they put their noses on one's knee, and seem to understand a lot of what one is feeling; but they can't make up for the person one is missing.

Still, they are better than nothing, and provide sympathy in their silent way.

Dear Andrew, this brings you my human sympathy,

from your friend
Vita

The first part of the year 1961 brought a long gap in the correspondence. It was not until March that Vita wrote to Andrew again.

FAREWELL

March 27, 1961

Dearest Andrew

I cannot remember when I last wrote to you. I have
been living in such a confusion of servant difficulties (illness) and trying against time to finish something for a publisher, and having 'flu myself, and my secretary not yet
back (she goes away from December till end of March)
that I haven't known where to turn. But I do know that I
haven't thanked you for the Peppermint sticks, and I do so
now, *most* gratefully. Too early to plant them, although
we have had a wonderful spring. The daffodils are a sight
to be seen. We had thieves after them the other night,
who swiped whole bunches of them, and if my little dog
hadn't heard something and barked I really believe they
would have had the lot. Several other gardens round here
were robbed likewise. It is probably gipsies, who resell the
flowers. I could have murdered them.

The thing I was trying to finish for a publisher is about
dogs; there are some really wonderful photographs of dogs
and I undertook to write the text—deadline April 1st,
which now of course I shan't be able to stick to, and I do
hate letting people down. But this wretched 'flu has
knocked a whole week out of life. I am better and hope to
get up in a day or two, but I have to be extra careful or it
might turn to virus pneumonia again, which has wrecked
my last two summers.

I thought of you when I was doing the poodle photograph. This one was of a miniature poodle: are yours large
or small? I am afraid I rather made fun of it, probably
because the only two miniatures I have ever known were

(111)

spoilt, odious little brutes. More the fault of their owners than their own faults. These miniatures are only apt to fall into the hands of silly women who don't know how to treat a dog.

It is such a lovely evening, and I do long to be out.

How are things going with you? I am so afraid you must feel very lonely now without your Walter. No doubt you have many friends, but it's not the same thing as a friend you share everything with in daily life.

Your young President has got his hands full and no mistake. But he is said to be possessed of boundless energy—I must say he makes a very good impression on me so far. But what a job!

Well—do write to me, dear Andrew, and say my silence is forgiven. I really *have* been in a mess.

Love
Vita

Despite his bereavement, Andrew wrote to Vita as usual of the little everyday occurrences of his life that he knew would interest her, including his poodle's enormous litter of ten pups. He also continued to look for newspaper clippings to enclose with his letters. In July she replied to him:

How are Savez-vous' surviving puppies? Fancy having 10!

You sent me a cutting about Susie, which interested me very much, and . . . a cutting about the death of my American aunt, (not step-mother.) She was a horrid woman, and we all loathed her. Now that she is no longer there, I go to Knole again; I hadn't been there for over 30 years, since my father died. I am very fond of my uncle, and he used to come and see me here, but I now see him at Knole. He is 91, and very frail, but as loveable and charming as ever.

It was the greatest (and perhaps the only) tragedy of Vita's life that she, as a woman, could not inherit her ancestral home and birthplace, the fantastical Knole House in Sevenoaks, Kent. As the only child from the union of Sackville-West cousins, she seemed to possess an indisputable right to the house, totally apart from her emotional bond to it. Her son Nigel wrote that Knole was like a lover to her. When her father died in 1930, the estate went by law to his brother Charles. Vita's antipathy for his wife prevented her from visiting the house she loved until after Lady Sackville's death in January 1961. Among the papers at Sissinghurst is the manuscript of a poem that expresses her feelings at being separated from Knole.

DIARY POEM[25]

My heart is broken against grey stone,
Against the Kentish Rag.
Smashed against it as ships in wreck
Smash on a Cornish crag.

Cracked is my heart and cannot mend;
It broke twelve years ago;
Never, never, never again
Shall I call my heart my own.

My heart was torn from my broken breast
And thrown against the stone—
The stone of my own friendly home
That broke it in the end.

Never, never, never to mend;
A smash that never heals;

Oh sorrow, that the thing I love
Should be the thing that kills.

Knole, you would not have broken me?
Me, passionate and wild?
You loved me, surely, in so far
As stone can love its child?

Knole, when I went from you, you missed
One of your many children, specially?
God knows I gave you all my love, my agony,
Scarcely a stone of you I had not kissed.

Knole! Knole! I stretch my hands to you in prayer,
You, grey and solid; you, enduring, staid;
You do not know what surges beat against your walls;
Miss me a little, I who am your soul.

The remainder of the letter Vita wrote on July 9 dealt with more commonplace events, the local flower show and the yearly influx of summer visitors to her Sissinghurst garden.

I wish you could have seen our village flower show yesterday. It is such an absolutely English thing,—couldn't be anywhere else. All the villagers exhibit, and the children have a fancy dress parade, and I open the show and in the evening I give away the prizes and present a silver cup (which I have to provide) and Harold draws the raffle and somebody wins a live pig. And there are side-shows, and a band, and it is all great fun.

We have had a lot of your countrymen-and-women here this year; they are always so nice and appreciative and seem to like my garden. Visitors pay one-and-sixpence entrance, which enables me to pay the wages and keep the garden up. I couldn't do it otherwise, and I really don't mind people wandering about.

She wrote again in September to report to Andrew about *Faces*, the book of dog photographs that she had told him about in March.

It comes out in November and I will send you a copy, though you will be very angry with me about what I say about poodles. (It applies to *miniature* poodles, though, which I don't think yours are.) You will realise that it is only a joke book; it just amused me writing the text for the excellent photographs. I learnt a lot about dogs in the process.

In this letter again her thoughts turned to the separation of life partners. She wondered:

Dear Andrew, how are you getting on in your now rather lonely life? You must miss your companion dreadfully. I think of you often, and wonder how you manage. It must leave such an awful gap, with stabs of memory throughout the day. I think one of the worst things about losing a life's companion like that, is constantly thinking "Oh, how that would have amused him!" or "Oh, I must tell him that," and then remembering that he isn't there to tell.

Andrew, with his usual optimistic spirit, wrote to reassure Vita about the condition of his life. She replied on October 29.

I am so glad that my worry about you missing your Walter unbearably was misplaced. It is wonderful of you to be able to feel him still there; and you must have a wonderful character to be able to feel that way. I should miss the physical presence so much, and not being able to talk and have the little jokes one shares in daily life.

Enough of that.

I shall now write about dogs.

I had to put my little Dan (collie) to sleep. He had become hysterical, and took to biting people. There was no choice left to me, but it cracked my heart, and I never forget him. However, my principle has always been that if you lose your dog, you must instantly replace him, so I telephoned to a breeder of golden retrievers—and she brought two puppies for me to choose from—and oh Andrew! must I confess? I fell for them, and bought them *both*. It was a crazy thing to do—but I don't regret it. They are angelic, but as they are only three months old they are

of course a handful. Talk about men being henpecked . . . I am puppy ridden, and my life is no longer my own.

By the way, I have told my publishers to send you a book called *Faces*—Photographs of dogs, with the text written by me. You won't like what I say about poodles; but it is *miniature* poodles I wrote about, not the larger sort like yours. The book isn't coming out till November 13th so don't expect it too soon especially as it will be sent by surface mail.

The photographs are grand—the text is just a joke, and not to be taken seriously.

Politics once again intruded into their correspondence. She concluded her letter:

I won't write about the state of the world. Neither you nor I can do anything about it, and meanwhile as Voltaire so wisely remarked, "One must cultivate one's garden," which I suppose means that one must live one's own life and make the best of it and be as charitable as one can in a Christian way to one's neighbors.

Love from
Vita

Voltaire seems to have been much in Vita's thoughts that autumn. The previous month she had written to Harold:

It's so hot, and I think of you in London and of poor Mr. Hammarskjöld dead in Katanga, and of all the poor people in the U.N. who must be so upset and worried. Meanwhile I go on with my futile little occupations. I've put 400 bulbs in the orchard (fritillaries which you despise, *Narcissus cyclamineus* which you like, *Ornithogalum* which is supposed to naturalise itself but which I have never yet induced to grow, and *Narcissus* 'La Riante'). It sometimes seems rather silly, but as Voltaire wisely remarked, *Il faut cultiver notre jardin.* It is really better to have created a *jardin* which gives pleasure to us as well as to many other people, than for me to go and sit down in Trafalgar Square.[26]

Vita's Christmas letter to Andrew was rather different in 1961 than it had been in previous years. Andrew had been in the habit of sending Vita American cigarettes. He had not known that his gift caused her great difficulties. She finally brought herself to explain the situation to him. Foremost in her mind, however, was the human situation of loneliness. So she opened her letter of December 18, 1961:

Dearest Andrew

It is time I wrote to you for Christmas and I do so with all my heartfelt wishes to you. You say you do not feel lonely without your Mr. Walter but I can't believe that you don't miss him a lot in a human way, although you may have this conviction of his presence in a spiritual way. Whichever way it is, dear Andrew, I try to understand it.

. . . .

I am glad my little Christmas present of *Faces*, the dog-book, arrived in good time. I can't tell you anything about Laelia Goehr who took the photographs, except that she is the widow of a musician called Walter Goehr, who was apparently quite well-known. I really don't know her at all, except in connection with her photographs for this book.

Now listen, Andrew, this is a difficult thing to say, and I hate having to say it, but I am having trouble with the Customs about the Kent cigarettes you have so very generously sent me. Hitherto, I have just paid the duty to the postman who delivered the parcel at the door, but this time I have received an alarming form to fill up from her Majesty's Customs and Excise, Paragraph 1 of the 7th Schedule, headed *Notice of Seizure*, and demanding extra payment "as a condition of waiver of seizure." It sounds very mediaeval, doesn't it? I am sure *waiver of seizure* must go back to the thirteenth century at least.

I like the phrase, but I think we should perhaps interpret it as meaning that you shouldn't send me any more Kent cigarettes. You wouldn't like me to be put in prison, would you?

Much love for Christmas and the whole of 1962,

from Vita

Much distressed, Andrew immediately wrote to Vita over his chagrin at the disasters incumbent upon his present. She answered him in January.

Please don't give another thought to the cigarettes; perhaps I shouldn't have told you. After all, I *had* them; and the duty only amounted to what I should have paid for them in a shop. It was only when the Customs started threatening to *fine* me that I refused!

A joke to make you laugh. A telegram arrived signed

Andrew, and was handed to Harold. It said "Would you read a manuscript and give me your opinion?" Harold was much puzzled as the only Andrew he could think of was the Duke of Devonshire. So he brought it to me saying "Perhaps this is from *your* Andrew? It is most unlikely that Andrew Devonshire would ask me or you to read a manuscript."

We sorted it out in the end.

The rest of the letter, aside from a complaint about the cold ("The water in my bedroom flower vases froze.") contained her usual notation of the itinerary of the Nicolsons' winter cruise. This year they were bound for the Caribbean. Her letter ended poignantly and ironically: "I will wave a hand to you across the ocean. May 1962 be kind to you all through its twelve months. Love, Vita."

On February 10, from on board the ship *Antilles*, Vita wrote Andrew her last real letter. By that time she had had intimations of the cancer that was to kill her. The entire cruise was darkened by her illness, which began on the train ride from London to meet the ship in Southampton.

Dearest Andrew

We are on our way home, across a grey tossing Atlantic, and should get to Southampton on the 15th, calling at Lisbon on the way. I can't say that this trip has been much of a success from my point of view, partly because I didn't like the West Indies, and partly because I was ill most of the time—I got bronchitis, and then I kept on getting fever,—all very tiresome and wasteful. You will wonder why I didn't like the West Indies which everybody raves

Andrew in 1974. *Courtesy of Michel Chalufour.*

about,—well, for one thing it isn't the sort of scenery I like, not austere enough, and for another thing it is all so terribly laid on for tourists and millionaires,—one has the impression of posh hotels everywhere, even if one doesn't go into them, and of dreadful people drinking cocktails all day.

In fact, it may be Nature's paradise, but it has been heavily corrupted by man.

The ship is quite all right: the food very good, but the cabins poky and ill equipped. We have some friends on board, with whom we have travelled before; and my closest friend has come too; I don't know if I've mentioned her to you, Edie Lamont;[27] she is a painter, also a very good gardener, and lives about 10 miles from Sissinghurst. Evelyn Waugh is also on board; he is amusing, but I have never liked him very much though I love his books. He can be so devastatingly rude to people, and I don't like that. This isn't personal, as he has never been anything but most amiable to me.

I am rather longing to get home, to my golden puppy and my garden, all the more so as I haven't been able to do any writing on board this time, I've felt too stupid. It was nice and warm in the tropics; that's one thing, but not much good if you have to spend half the time in bed in your cabin.

I've forgotten to say I got your two letters, bless you. I've been awfully bad at writing letters; I really just went hopelessly flop, and shall get into trouble with my friends at home.

There was a gala dinner the other night, and the chef

made a life-size poodle, all in solid white sugar. I thought
of you and how it would amuse you.

> With love
> V.

Her illness, of course, was not due only to bronchitis. She
returned to Sissinghurst on February 15. She was operated on
for cancer of the stomach in London on March 1. Bravely she
dictated her last letter to Andrew on April 10. On June 2 she
died peacefully at Sissinghurst.

Dearest Andrew

I am sure you will be sorry to hear that I have been very
ill and had to have a big operation. That is why I have not
answered you for such a long time, and even now I have
to dictate a letter. I was in hospital, but have managed to
get home at last.

I will write to you myself as soon as I am able, but this
is just to let you know what has been happening, and to
thank you for the coloured photographs, which were so
pretty.

Don't worry about me now, as I am going to be quite all
right.

> Yours ever
> Vita

Notes

1. Harold Nicolson, *Diaries and Letters 1939–1945* (New York: Atheneum, 1967), p. 472.
2. The book she referred to was *In Your Garden*.
3. Harold Nicolson, *Diaries and Letters 1945–1962* (New York: Atheneum, 1968), p. 195. Hereafter referred to as HN, *Diaries III*.
4. The abbreviation stands for Knight Commander of the Royal Victorian Order.
5. HN, *Diaries III*, p. 244.
6. HN, *Diaries III*, p. 219.
7. V. Sackville-West, "June 2nd, 1953," *The Times Literary Supplement*, 5 June 1953, p. 358. This is one of the very few published poems of Vita's later years.
8. Letter from V. Sackville-West to Andrew Reiber, April 25, 1954.
9. HN, *Diaries III*, p. 245.
10. *Ibid.*, p. 250.
11. V. Sackville-West, "Evening," *Collected Poems* (London: The Hogarth Press, 1933), p. 166.
12. "The Squire" was the pet name given to Walter Sinclair by his friends.
13. The inscription read "For Andrew, via Ann, and signed by Vita—at Sissinghurst on July 20, 1954."
14. Vita muddled the name. She corrected herself on a later postcard to Andrew: "It wasn't Harvard that my son went to, it was HAVERFORD."
15. Sir Winston Churchill was then Prime Minister.
16. HN, *Diaries III*, p. 276.
17. *Ibid.*, p. 280.
18. *Ibid.*, p. 284.
19. The President of the Royal Horticultural Society in 1956 was David Bowes-Lyon.

20. HN, *Diaries III*, p. 319.
21. Harold Nicolson, *Journey to Java* (London: Constable, 1957), pp. 182–83.
22. *Ibid.*, p. 187.
23. The erythronium is commonly known in the United States as the dog-tooth violet.
24. HN, *Diaries III*, p. 386.
25. The poem was first published in Michael Stevens, V. *Sackville-West, A Critical Biography* (New York: Scribners, 1974), pp. 149–50. First published by Michael Joseph Ltd., London, 1973.
26. HN, *Diaries III*, p. 398.
27. Edie Lamont shared many of Vita's interests, such as gardening and dogs. She was one of Vita's closest friends in her last years and still lives in Kent.

References

Nicolson, Harold. *Diaries and Letters 1939–1945*. New York: Atheneum, 1967.

———. *Diaries and Letters 1945–1962*. New York: Atheneum, 1968.

———. *Journey to Java*. London: Constable, 1957.

Sackville-West, Vita. *Collected Poems*. London: The Hogarth Press, 1933.

———. Letters to Andrew Reiber, 1951–1962.

Stevens, Michael. V. *Sackville-West, A Critical Biography*. New York: Scribners, 1974. (London: Michael Joseph, 1975).

U-11

95

AR 41